INTERNATIONAL DEVELOPMENT IN FOCUS

A New Dawn for Global Value Chain Participation in the Philippines

GUILLERMO ARENAS AND SOULEYMANE COULIBALY, EDITORS

WORLD BANK GROUP

Contents

Box

Figures

Tables

Foreword

In the 1990s, innovations in information and communication technology and logistics, along with lower tariff barriers, allowed global firms to offshore parts of their production, giving rise to global value chains (GVCs). Parts and components began moving across regions and the globe as lead global firms looked for efficiencies wherever they could find them. GVC growth was mostly concentrated in machinery, electronics, and transportation and in the regions specializing in those sectors: East Asia and Pacific, North America, and Western Europe. GVC participation has stimulated productivity growth in these regions through knowledge spillovers, access to a larger variety of imported inputs, economies of scale, and specialization in firms' core activities.

Yet, despite these benefits, GVC and trade growth has slowed in recent years. The deceleration is driven by the decline in global growth and investment, increases in protectionism, and the slowing pace of trade reforms. Moreover, it is affected by the emergence of new technologies of production, such as automation, and by new technologies of distribution, such as digital platforms, both of which are creating risks and opportunities for GVCs and trade.

Risks and opportunities have been further accentuated by the COVID-19 (coronavirus) pandemic, as we see across the East Asia and Pacific region. As the pandemic disrupted trade flows and GVC configuration, in agreement with the government of the Philippines the World Bank put together a team of experienced macroeconomic, trade, and investment experts and tasked them to work with the Department of Trade and Industry, the National Economic and Development Authority, the Department of Finance, and relevant industry associations to explore ways to turn this crisis into an opportunity for the country.

This book is the product of that collaboration. It provides policy recommendations to increase the Philippines' participation in GVCs in a post-COVID-19 world. The book uses up-to-date trade data, analysis of megatrends affecting selected value chains, and interviews with multinational companies and their local suppliers to inform a strategic approach to rethink, diversify, and reorient the country's GVC participation.

The book also explores policies to mobilize key stakeholders (government, lead firms, and domestic suppliers) and to foster greater participation in three strategic GVC clusters: industrial, manufacturing, and transportation; technology, media, and telecommunications; and health and life sciences. Guided by this strategic orientation, we look forward to supporting the Philippines' recovery from COVID-19 and its reversion to a high-growth path to achieve *Ambisyon Natin* 2040.

Ceferino "Perry" Rodolfo
Undersecretary for the Industry Development and Trade Policy Group
Department of Trade and Industry
Government of the Philippines

Hassan Zaman
Director, East Asia and Pacific Region
Equitable Growth, Finance, and Institutions Global Practice
The World Bank

Ndiamé Diop
Country Director for Brunei, Malaysia, the Philippines, and Thailand
The World Bank

Acknowledgments

This study was prepared by a team co-led by Souleymane Coulibaly (program leader, EEADR) and Guillermo Arenas (economist, ETIRI) and comprising Angella Faith Montfaucon (economist, EEAM2), Natnael Simachew Nigatu (consultant, EEAM2), Kevin Chua (senior economist, EEAM2), Yan Liu (economist, ETICI), Victor Steenbergen (economist, ETICI), Gerlin May U. Catangui (senior economist, ETICI), and David Brown (consultant, ETICI). Valuable comments were received from Jaime Frias (senior economist, EEAF2), Jin Lee (economist, EEAF2), Richard Record (lead economist, EEAM2), Rong Qian (senior economist, EEAM2), Ian Gillson (lead economist, ETIRI), Michael Ferrantino (lead economist, ETIRI), Asya Akhlaque (lead economist, EEAF2), Massimiliano Cali (senior economist, EEAM2), and Shafaat Khan (economist, EAPCE). Excellent team support was provided by Elysse Miranda and Kristiana Rosario (EACPF). Management oversight was received from Lars Christian Moller (practice manager, EEAM2), Cecile Niang (practice manager, EEAF2), Hassan Zaman (regional director, EEADR), Ndiamé Diop (country director, EACPF), and Victoria Kwakwa (regional vice president, EAPVP).

The team thanks the Department of Trade and Industry for the excellent collaboration, including organizing two roundtables with key stakeholders and facilitating access to key information and data. Special thanks go to the Philippine Board of Investments and the Philippine Economic Zone Authority for being the liaison with key private operators and professional associations. Excellent comments received from the Department of Finance and the National Economic and Development Authority on the final version of this study are acknowledged.

About the Editors and Contributors

EDITORS

Guillermo Arenas is an economist in the Trade and Regional Integration Unit at the World Bank. His area of expertise covers various aspects of international economics and public policy, including trade policy, export competitiveness, and impact evaluation. Arenas specializes in the microeconomic analysis of trade and fiscal policies using firm-level data. He holds an MPA from Syracuse University (United States).

Souleymane Coulibaly is the lead economist and program leader for the Equitable Growth, Finance, and Institutions Practice Group for Brunei, Malaysia, the Philippines, and Thailand at the World Bank. Before moving to Manila, he was the program leader and lead economist for Central Africa. Coulibaly's publications and ongoing research deal with the impact of geography on firms' location, trade flows, and regional integration. Coulibaly was a coauthor of *World Development Report 2009: Reshaping Economic Geography*, contributed to the *Global Economic Prospects* Overview and Global Outlook (2005), and has written many papers published in peer-reviewed journals as well as three World Bank books: *Diversified Urbanization: The Case of Côte d'Ivoire* (2016); *Eurasian Cities: New Realities along the Silk Road* (2012); and *Trade Expansion through Market Connection: The Central Asian Markets of Kazakhstan, Kyrgyz Republic, and Tajikistan* (2011). He recently coedited the World Bank book *Africa in the New Trade Environment: Market Access in Troubled Times* (2021). Coulibaly, an Ivoirian national, holds a double PhD in international trade and economic geography from the University of Paris 1 Panthéon-Sorbonne (France) and the University of Lausanne (Switzerland).

CONTRIBUTORS

David Brown is an investment policy and promotion consultant at the World Bank Group. His areas of expertise cover competitiveness, global value chain dynamics, sustainable economic development, and links enabling spillovers from foreign direct investment to benefit local small and medium enterprises and entrepreneurs. He has broad sectoral experience in areas such as mobility and knowledge-based productive cluster development. He was recently the team leader and coauthor of *The Future of the EU Automotive Industry*, published by the European Parliament in November 2021, and holds an MBA with distinction from the University of Liverpool (United Kingdom).

Gerlin May U. Catangui is a senior economist in the Investment Climate Unit of the Trade, Investment, and Competitiveness Department at the World Bank. She develops projects and provides analytical and policy advisory in the design and implementation of projects and operations focused on investment, global value chains, firm internationalization, and competitiveness, especially in the East Asia and Pacific, Middle East and North Africa, and South Asia regions. Catangui recently contributed to the *2021 Development Policy Financing Retrospective: Facing Crisis, Fostering Recovery*. She holds an MBA in public service (international development) from the University of Birmingham (United Kingdom) and a master's in public policy from the National University of Singapore.

Kevin Chua is a senior economist in the Macroeconomics, Trade, and Investment Global Practice at the World Bank Philippines office. His fields of specialization include macroeconomics, monetary economics, and international trade, and his publications and research cover topics on international value chains, export competitiveness, and regional integration. Chua coauthored the book *The Asian Noodle Bowl: Free Trade and Economic Integration in the Post-Crisis Era* (2015) and has written in peer-reviewed journals on revealed comparative advantage, international production chains, and the evolving trade links between the Association of Southeast Asian Nations and China. He holds a PhD in economics from Fordham University and a master's degree in international affairs from Columbia University (both United States).

Yan Liu is an economist in the Investment Climate Unit at the World Bank. Her areas of expertise cover empirical research and policy advisory related to foreign direct investment, global value chains, firm productivity and innovation, and structural transformation. Liu coauthored the book *An Investment Perspective on Global Value Chains* (2021). She holds a PhD in economics from Peking University (China).

Angella Faith Montfaucon, a Malawian national, is in the Macroeconomics, Trade and Investment Global Practice at the World Bank. Her work includes trade, trade policy, fiscal policy, and World Bank operations. Before joining the World Bank, she worked at the Reserve Bank of Malawi in private sector banking; she also has university teaching experience. She has published in peer-reviewed journals on exchange rate pass-though, tariff and nontariff measures, microeconomics of international trade, and financial inclusion. Montfaucon joined the World Bank in the 2019 cohort of the Young Professionals program. She holds a PhD in economics from Yokohama National University (Japan) and an MA in economic policy management from the University of Zambia.

Natnael Simachew Nigatu is a consultant in the Macroeconomics, Trade, and Investment Global Practice at the World Bank. His research focuses on the intersections of international trade and labor economics. Before joining the Bank, he worked as a postdoctoral researcher at Lund University (Sweden), where he taught advanced courses in economic integration, and he has been a visiting scholar at Purdue University (United States). Nigatu holds a bachelor's degree in economics from Bahir Dar University (Ethiopia) and a master's degree and a PhD in economics from the University of Copenhagen (Denmark).

Victor Steenbergen is an economist in the Investment Climate Unit at the World Bank. His area of experience relates to quantitative policy research and analysis, particularly related to foreign direct investment, trade, and tax policy. He recently coauthored *An Investment Perspective on Global Value Chains* (2021) and *Making the Most of the African Continental Free Trade Area: Leveraging Trade and Foreign Direct Investment to Boost Growth and Poverty Reduction* (2022). Steenbergen joined the World Bank in 2018. Before that, he provided longer-term technical assistance to the governments of Malawi, Mexico, Nigeria, and Rwanda. He holds a master's degree in public administration and development economics from the London School of Economics (United Kingdom).

Executive Summary

INTRODUCTION

This book provides policy recommendations to increase the Philippines' participation in global value chains (GVCs) in a post-COVID-19 (coronavirus) world. The Philippines could benefit from the shifting dynamics of GVCs by attracting more investments as investors look for alternative production sources less sensitive to trade tensions. The book uses trade data, analysis of megatrends, and interviews with multinational companies and their local suppliers to inform a strategic approach to the country's GVC participation. The main finding is that the crisis can help strengthen the country's foreign direct investment attractiveness and motivate operators in GVCs to develop the skills they need to participate more advantageously in GVCs. The book also explores policies to mobilize key stakeholders and foster participation in three strategic GVC clusters.

From an international trade perspective, the Philippines is known for its exports of electronics, business process outsourcing (BPO) services, and skilled nurses. For electronics and BPO, the Philippines specializes in intermediate exports. With an increasing comparative advantage over recent decades, the health care sector is a natural option for diversification, particularly given the threat and opportunities presented by the COVID-19 pandemic.

The Philippines has an opportunity to diversify into three GVC clusters that are being restructured by the COVID-19 pandemic. The first cluster is the industrial, manufacturing, and transportation (IMT) sector, for which the Philippines is positioned in the semiconductor, automotive, and aerospace segments. The second cluster is the technology, media, and telecommunications (TMT) cluster, for which the Philippines is positioned in the BPO segment. Before the rise in China-US trade tensions, TMT production had been moving to Mexico and Vietnam in response to the rising cost of labor in China and a desire to diversify production. The third cluster is the health and life sciences (HLS) sector, which is incipient in the Philippines. The HLS sector could take advantage of the return of health care workers during the COVID-19 crisis and emerging telehealth and telemedicine activities to complement the traditional BPO sector.

WHAT ARE THE OPPORTUNITIES FOR THE PHILIPPINES TO REPOSITION ITSELF IN GVCs?

Although COVID-19 significantly affected trade, foreign direct investment (FDI), and jobs in the three GVCs, it also created opportunities for the Philippines to reposition itself. In 2020, Philippine exports of goods and services contracted 15 percent, the most precipitous decline in at least 40 years. Electronics, the most important export sector, declined 8.8 percent versus 2019, with almost all of the main subsectors—semiconductors, computer parts, office equipment, and telecommunications—experiencing similar declines. The only service sector that experienced export growth was business services (0.6 percent).

FDI inflows also declined after the pandemic began. In 2020, the total approved FDI was only US$2 billion, down by more than 70 percent from US$7.5 billion in 2019. The decline in FDI was apparent across most industries and source countries. Greenfield FDI announcements also were significantly lower in 2020 than in the previous five years. COVID-19 disproportionally affected occupations and industries that require more personal and frequent interaction, like the arts, entertainment, and tourism sectors. On the upside, the pandemic led to a substantial increase in the number of trained information and communication technology (ICT) experts in many industries.

The advent of disruptive technologies, servicification of manufacturing, and strategic adjustments in supply chains are shaping global trade and GVCs, giving impetus for policy makers to respond. GVCs were undergoing structural changes even before the pandemic. Megatrends—including (a) the rise of automation and artificial intelligence, which erodes traditional comparative advantage based on low wages; (b) the use of services in manufacturing, which results in growing demand for high-skill labor; and (c) the regional concentration of goods production—have the potential to change the role of low- and middle-income countries in international production networks. The COVID-19 pandemic amplified the need for some of these changes and forced firms to address supply risk and diversification by (a) enhancing the digitalization of supply chains, which enables companies to react in a fast and flexible way to unexpected situations and to recover more quickly (resilience vs. efficiency); (b) diversifying their suppliers; and (c) building redundancy in their supply chains by holding larger inventories or building redundancy into transportation networks (just-in-case vs. just-in-time) (McKinsey Global Institute 2020).

The IMT cluster is exposed to these market forces. Three subsectors of the IMT cluster operate in the Philippines: aerospace, automotive, and semiconductors. Over the last decade, Asia Pacific was the fastest-growing region for airline activity, benefiting from introduction of the Boeing 787 Dreamliner, the production of which spurred a wide geographic spread of suppliers. The Philippines hosts the top aircraft interiors company in the world (Collins Aerospace) and the world's leading maintenance, repair, and overhaul company (Lufthansa Technik) but has been unable to attract other suppliers and expand the cluster. The switch from combustion engine to electric vehicles will be the main change in the automotive GVC. Automotive companies are committed to switching to electric vehicle manufacturing in the near future. This change, combined with increasing outward FDI by Chinese companies and the transition of some electronic assembly firms (for example, Foxconn) to electric vehicle assembly, will provide opportunities for the Philippines to enter the electric vehicle GVC. Finally, the semiconductor industry will benefit from the recent boost in digitalization during the COVID-19 pandemic, although outsourced semiconductor assembly and test, the segment present in the Philippines, is the most vulnerable to disruptive technologies. Vietnam is overtaking the Philippines in the electronics contract manufacturing segment. Increasing skills to undertake research and development functions could help to increase business for outsourced semiconductor assembly and test firms. The Philippines has an opportunity to upgrade its participation in the electronics and electrical parts and components GVCs, which link these three IMT subsectors. It could do so by attracting FDI in design capacity so that more value added is captured and manufacturing is retained and expanded.

Digitalization of services in the TMT cluster is also reshaping opportunities for the Philippines. The key trend for the BPO sector moving forward is the switch from cost saving to value addition. In the next decade, the BPO segment will support and contribute to the competitiveness and efficiency of other GVCs. Artificial intelligence–based cloud analytics and enterprise resource planning will continue, as will working from home. That 82 percent of BPO centers and shared services centers in the Philippines serve global markets is a very positive attribute that targeted policies can leverage to boost the country's participation in the TMT cluster.

With a health crisis at the root of the current global economic distress, the HLS cluster plays a strategic role in security, opening income-generating opportunities in all countries, including the Philippines. Over the next decade, multinational companies will continue to seek ways to manufacture medicines faster and more cheaply. Smaller, innovative, more agile companies will have a more important role in bringing medicines to market. The nascent state of life sciences and the biotechnology ecosystem in the Philippines is a major constraint to the growth of the biopharmaceutical sector. However, as pharmaceuticals, medical devices, and health care services become more integrated and the management of information, such as biometrics, becomes as important as the management of products, development of the IMT and TMT clusters could facilitate the emergence of an HLS cluster in the Philippines. The IMT cluster (through electronics parts and components) can reach the medical device sector, the TMT cluster (through health care information technology [IT] services) can reach the health care service sector, and the pharmaceutical sector can attract lead multinational companies while promoting a network of domestic suppliers. The big data and analytical needs associated with health care thereby represent additional opportunities for growth of BPO and IT outsourcing in the Philippines.

Addressing constraints on participation in the IMT, TMT, and HLS clusters will boost economic recovery and resilience in the post-COVID-19 world in the Philippines. The pandemic has exacerbated the country's structural challenges, such as restrictions on equity in network sectors and scarcity of advanced science, technology, engineering, and mathematics skills in the electronics and electrical, IT business processing management, and health care GVCs. The domestic value added in exports to key trading partners in these GVCs is smaller in the Philippines than in Malaysia, Thailand, and Vietnam and grew slowly during the past decade. Structural constraints have weighed on the country's participation in these GVCs. The Philippines relies heavily on China as a source and a destination for its GVC participation, which makes it vulnerable to disruptions caused by the fierce competition between China and the United States in the semiconductor sector and persistent trade tensions between these two leading economies. Furthermore, over the past decade, the Philippines has lagged behind its regional peers in attracting FDI, a key driver of technology and know-how for upgrading in these GVCs. At the same time, this crisis provides an opportunity to rethink, diversify, and redeploy the participation of the Philippines in three strategic clusters that are currently undergoing global reconfiguration.

HOW TO SEIZE THESE OPPORTUNITIES?

The *World Development Report 2020* provides a framework for analyzing the participation of the Philippines in the IMT, TMT, and HLS clusters. GVC participation is determined by fundamentals such as factor endowments, market size, geography, and institutional quality, differentiated by the level of development of each country (World Bank 2020). These cross-cutting opportunities and challenges can be grouped as institutions, infrastructure, and interventions. Institutions refer to cross-cutting policies and institutional reforms. Infrastructure refers to connectivity infrastructure. Interventions refer to targeted infrastructure and service provision in special economic zones and upgrading strategies. Choosing the right policies can shape each one of these fundamentals and foster the Philippines' GVC participation in the three clusters. As the country shifts gears for a post-COVID-19 recovery and seeks to maximize job creation, attract FDI, and raise export revenue, this book explores ways to mobilize key stakeholders (government, lead firms, and domestic suppliers). Table ES.1 summarizes proposed high-priority cross-cutting and cluster-specific policy actions.

The Philippines has an opportunity to undertake key economywide institutional actions in the short term. To address constraints on FDI attractiveness, the Philippine Congress amended in late 2021 and early 2022 three laws to foster liberalization. These are amendments to the Foreign Investments Act, the Retail Trade Liberalization Act, and the Public Service Act. These flagship laws should be complemented by adoption of the Open Access in Data Transmission Act to promote the digital economy and implementation of the Customs Modernization and Tariff Act (including establishment of the national single window). The implementing rules and regulations of the Corporate Recovery and Tax Incentives for Enterprise (CREATE) Act were issued in June 2021, but the immediate issuance of the Strategic Investments Priorities Plan by the Board of Investments is needed for full implementation of the law. Timely adoption of pending laws, their implementing rules and regulations, and the Strategic Investments Priorities Plan is essential for the Philippines to take advantage of GVC reconfiguration. Many of these actions involve the Department of Trade and Industry and the Board of Investments, together with sector regulators in the public sector and sector associations and lead firms in the private sector.

Over the medium term, attention could focus on filling the country's connectivity and energy gaps. The erosion of fiscal buffers during the COVID-19 pandemic means that a concerted effort is needed to raise the financing required to fill the country's infrastructure gap, focusing on connectivity (digital as well as physical) and securing access to a competitive and clean energy supply. Targeting special economic zones would signal the country's commitment to fostering a new dawn of GVC participation in strategic clusters and send a powerful signal to lead firms operating in these clusters. But, for inclusive, job-creating GVC participation, programs to encourage the participation of domestic suppliers should be promoted as well.

TABLE ES.1 Summary of high-priority cross-cutting and sector-specific policy actions for the Philippines

POLICY AREA	CONSTRAINTS	INSTITUTIONS CROSS-CUTTING POLICIES AND INSTITUTIONAL REFORMS	INFRASTRUCTURE POLICIES TO ADDRESS CONNECTIVITY CONSTRAINTS	INTERVENTIONS POLICIES TO FOSTER PARTICIPATION IN THE THREE CLUSTERSᵃ
Trade	• Overheads and bottlenecks associated with exporting, which have resulted in the largest contraction of exports in 40 years, despite a narrowing of the monthly trade imbalance to US$2.3 billion in February 2021	• Implement tariff commitments and harmonize rules of origin with RCEP members • Consider establishing preferential trade agreements with strategic trade partners to attract FDI in key clusters	• Fully implement the Customs Modernization and Tariff Act by establishing a national single window to facilitate trade and improve the overall competitiveness of the economy	
	• Propensity of pharmaceutical companies to serve regional markets rather than to export due to high trade costs, practicality, and profitability	• Enable domestic pharmaceutical companies to obtain US Food and Drug Administration approval		
Foreign direct investment	• Lack of investor confidence • Loss of competitiveness vis-à-vis competing locations (for example, Vietnam) • Inability of foreign investors to engage international trainers and mentors • Highest power costs in the region, with the exception of Japan • Investment promotion that was ill-equipped to attract the next generation of foreign investors • Growing concern of investors about the lack of policy on how the government wants industry to look by 2030	• Fully implement amendments to the Foreign Investments Act, the Retail Trade Liberalization Act, and the Public Service Act to boost FDI attractiveness in key sectors • Fully implement the CREATE Act through the immediate issuance of the Strategic Investments Priorities Plan • Reintroduce and adopt a Philippine sovereign wealth fund act		
	• Overdependence on imported inputs and raw materials • Inadequate contingency planning for investors supplying international customers just in time • Opacity of electric vehicle and associated infrastructure policy and timelines, dissuading investors from making medium- to long-term commitments		• Increase funding for telecommunications infrastructure within the infrastructure investment program via public-private partnerships and sovereign wealth funds	• Promote targeted investment: – Attract tier-two and tier-three suppliers to expand the base of suppliers for aeronautics and diversify from aircraft interiors

continued

TABLE ES.1, *continued*

		INSTITUTIONS	INFRASTRUCTURE	INTERVENTIONS
POLICY AREA	**CONSTRAINTS**	**CROSS-CUTTING POLICIES AND INSTITUTIONAL REFORMS**	**POLICIES TO ADDRESS CONNECTIVITY CONSTRAINTS**	**POLICIES TO FOSTER PARTICIPATION IN THE THREE CLUSTERS[a]**
	• Dependence of the EMS segment on intermediary products and "sunset" products nearing the end of their commercial life cycle • Lack of a biopharmaceutical and life sciences ecosystem • Insufficient investment in telecommunications infrastructure that undermines digitalization • Slow pace of transitioning the BPO segment from cost saving to value addition			– Leverage electronics strengths by enabling EMS companies to transition into electric vehicle assembly, component manufacture, and charging infrastructure – Develop the Philippines as a center of excellence for semiconductor design – Leverage the success of global shared services centers to attract investment in IT outsourcing and knowledge process outsourcing – Motivate multinational pharmaceutical companies in the Philippines to outsource contract manufacturing to local companies
Skills	• Insufficient skills upgrading within the services sector • Lack of workers with skills required by innovation firms, with about 80% of respondents citing lack of commitment and poor communication and technical skills as impediments	• Amend profession-specific laws to encourage FDI and attract skilled workers in targeted segments (that is, remove "practice of professions" from the Foreign Investments Act and the foreign investment negative list and amend applicable sector or professional regulations) • Simplify work permits and visas to maximize labor mobility and skills provision • Conclude mutual recognition arrangements on professional services in the RCEP to liberalize professional mobility	• Assess the country's internet infrastructure (quality and reliability of internet connection) and expand it to support training programs effectively	• Strengthen industry-academia links to bridge the gaps in workforce capacity building and skills development

continued

TABLE ES.1, *continued*

		INSTITUTIONS	INFRASTRUCTURE	INTERVENTIONS
POLICY AREA	**CONSTRAINTS**	**CROSS-CUTTING POLICIES AND INSTITUTIONAL REFORMS**	**POLICIES TO ADDRESS CONNECTIVITY CONSTRAINTS**	**POLICIES TO FOSTER PARTICIPATION IN THE THREE CLUSTERS**[a]
		• Fully operationalize the Philippine Qualifications Framework to harmonize and facilitate seamless progression from different levels of education and training, promote skills upgrading and lifelong learning, and be on par with international standards		
	• Very high staff attrition rates within BPO segment before COVID-19 • Within ICT and financial services, shortage of skills and low backward participation in GVCs • Insufficient recognition within the Department of Trade and Industry's AI Road Map that the uptake of AI is slower than in competing countries • Scarcity of workers with advanced skills to support scalability	• Fast-track implementation of the AI Road Map • Conduct a technical skills gap analysis to provide concrete recommendations for reskilling and retooling policies for the three clusters • Expand the provision of and access to online ICT-related education and training courses and the Commission on Higher Education's Service Management (Advanced) Program for BPO centers	• Increase the supply of engineering skills with appropriate (sector-specific) certification • Ensure that the CREATE Act motivates the private sector to upskill personnel through training grants • Develop sectoral skills policy frameworks that are responsive to fast-changing requirements aligned with global standards • Support sector-specific online job fairs	
GVC integration	• Low productivity of small and medium firms compared with larger firms • Difficulty meeting international quality standards • Difficulty accessing markets • High costs to serve the domestic market given the country's archipelagic state • Inadequacies in business operation, such as lack of proper facilities and access to relevant technologies • Fragmentation of full support services to small and medium enterprises • Large gaps in the entrepreneurial ecosystem	• Prioritize the adoption and adaptation of existing new technologies over R&D to improve the access of small and medium enterprises to new technology • Address constraints on small and medium enterprises in accessing finance, such as the ineffective public credit guarantee scheme for small and medium firms and inefficient insolvency regimes		

continued

TABLE ES.1, *continued*

		INSTITUTIONS	INFRASTRUCTURE	INTERVENTIONS
POLICY AREA	**CONSTRAINTS**	**CROSS-CUTTING POLICIES AND INSTITUTIONAL REFORMS**	**POLICIES TO ADDRESS CONNECTIVITY CONSTRAINTS**	**POLICIES TO FOSTER PARTICIPATION IN THE THREE CLUSTERS**[a]
		• Complete an entrepreneurship ecosystem audit to promote an innovation ecosystem in cities and special economic zones hosting targeted segments • Conduct reverse trade fairs for multinational corporations located in the Philippines to source more inputs locally		
	• Reluctance of small and medium enterprises to engage with multinational corporations wanting to source locally			• Attract tier-one and tier-two suppliers to create greater opportunities for GVC integration by local small and medium enterprises
Sector competitiveness	• Gaps in the range and quality of services, which undermines manufacturing performance and market accessibility • Risk aversion of local conglomerates, which are more interested in trading than in manufacturing and are content to serve the domestic market	• Formulate and endorse a policy statement on the IMT cluster to boost investor confidence • Develop and strengthen cluster dynamics to increase the services content of goods	• Continue to implement the Common Tower Policy to increase private investment in ICT • Adopt and implement the Open Access in Data Transmission Act to promote the digital economy	

	• Inability of productivity and innovation spillovers from FDI and domestic multinational corporations to sustain improved competitiveness
	• Need for a new, more export-oriented electric vehicle model to develop the automotive sector, as the CARS Program has not achieved the desired impact
	• For electronics, a positive but modest trade balance and exceptionally low value added, with food processing, for example, generating twice the value added as electronics
		• Within the IMT cluster policy, articulate the following:
		  – How the aerospace, automobile, and electronics industry will look by 2030
		  – Parameters of a core electric vehicle policy, including when all new vehicles sold must be electric or hybrid, a charging infrastructure for electric vehicles, and a time frame for monetization
		  – An electronics policy elaborating how the Philippines will emerge as a center of excellence for semiconductor design and electric vehicle electronics
			• Leverage the country's strengths in electronics to design, build, and export electric vehicle charging infrastructure	• Conduct a GVC reconfiguration analysis of companies to support stronger cluster links
				• Develop a five-year plan to develop and upgrade GVCs in the three clusters

continued

TABLE ES.1, *continued*

POLICY AREA	CONSTRAINTS	INSTITUTIONS CROSS-CUTTING POLICIES AND INSTITUTIONAL REFORMS	INFRASTRUCTURE POLICIES TO ADDRESS CONNECTIVITY CONSTRAINTS	INTERVENTIONS POLICIES TO FOSTER PARTICIPATION IN THE THREE CLUSTERS[a]

	• An embryonic biopharma-ceutical and life sciences sector that lacks a core, a champion, and a cluster culture
	• Overdependence of aerospace exports on Airbus and Boeing; insufficient focus on supplying leading aerospace companies in the Asia Pacific region and in China
	• Lag in BPO and IT-enabled services with regard to IT outsourcing, knowledge process outsourcing, and capitalizing on surges in health care BPO centers
		– A policy and strategic direction for converting the Philippines' natural resources in quartz and copper oxide into lithium-ion batteries for electric vehicles and copper for electric vehicle motors
		• Align TMT policy with the AI Road Map
		  – Unlock the GVC efficiency gains of the verticals (sectors) being supported by BPO centers
		  – Continue decreasing "Manila-centricity" for BPO centers to the extent that the business case will allow
		• Fill the HLS policy vacuum by elevating the Philippine Pharma Road Map under preparation to an HLS policy:
		  – Accelerate develop-ment of the life science and biotechnology cluster by developing (a) a knowledge center of excellence, (b) an innovation ecosys-tem, and (c) a superior enabling environment with, for example, a dedicated technology park or campus and venture capital provision		

continued

TABLE ES.1, *continued*

POLICY AREA	CONSTRAINTS	INSTITUTIONS	INFRASTRUCTURE	INTERVENTIONS
		CROSS-CUTTING POLICIES AND INSTITUTIONAL REFORMS	POLICIES TO ADDRESS CONNECTIVITY CONSTRAINTS	POLICIES TO FOSTER PARTICIPATION IN THE THREE CLUSTERS[a]
		– Ensure that the Philippine Food and Drug Administration can streamline and accelerate a new drug-approval process, while resolving the lack of bioequivalence exposure within the Philippines		

Source: World Bank staff.
Note: Color code: light blue = economy wide, light green = cluster specific. AI = artificial intelligence; BPO = business process outsourcing; CARS = Comprehensive Automotive Resurgence Strategy; CREATE = Corporate Recovery and Tax Incentives for Enterprises; EMS = electronics manufacturing services; FDI = foreign direct investment; GVC = global value chain; HLS = health and life sciences; ICT = information and communication technology; IMT = industrial, manufacturing, and transportation; IT = information technology; R&D = research and development; RCEP = Regional Comprehensive Economic Partnership; TMT = technology, media, and telecommunication.
a. Including targeted infrastructure and upgrading of investor-trader service provision.

Interviews with lead firms and domestic firms operating in these three clusters provide preliminary insights into sector- and cluster-specific reforms. Given the commonalities affecting the competitiveness of aerospace, automotive, and electronics, the next steps for the IMT cluster could be to use the GVC reconfiguration policy dialogue initiated by this study as the focal point for an IMT policy for the 2030 horizon. For the TMT cluster, the next steps could focus on motivating and enabling existing BPO centers to upgrade into big data and analytics and accelerating the acquisition of skills to build on the Philippines' shared services center successes in supporting global operations. For the HLS cluster, a policy framework is needed to accelerate the transition of the pharmaceutical industry into a vibrant, innovative biopharmaceutical industry by 2030, centered on leveraging US Food and Drug Administration approval and certification to open doors to key export markets. Three prerequisites are essential for a successful biotechnology and life sciences cluster: (a) a knowledge center of excellence, (b) an innovation ecosystem (skills, research and development funding, venture capital, and specialist services), and (c) a life sciences technology park, given the correlation between dedicated zones and successful biotech clusters in Boston, Cambridge, Edinburgh, Munich, San Francisco, and Singapore.

The challenges that lie ahead after the COVID-19 pandemic have given the Philippines a unique opportunity to align policies, improve the business climate, speed the pace of reform, and create a policy and institutional framework. Policies are needed to strengthen the country's position in key GVCs and to take advantage of opportunities as they arise. Decisive policy action that channels investment into priority sustainable development sectors has never been so critical. Although changing GVC dynamics is beyond the power of most governments, understanding future trends in GVCs and drivers of change would enable the government to anticipate and respond to those changes better by realigning existing or crafting new investment policies to maximize the benefits from any GVC reconfiguration.

POSTSCRIPT: GVC RAMIFICATIONS OF THE WAR IN UKRAINE

At the time of this book's publication, the war in Ukraine is unfolding with a rapidly mounting humanitarian cost. It is unclear how the conflict will end. What is clear is that the loss of life is unprecedented in over a half century in Europe. What is also clear is that the GVC clusters, which are undergoing a COVID pandemic-induced reconfiguration, will also face mounting pressure to anticipate and respond to shifting supply-side dynamics as a consequence of the conflict.

Although the semiconductor supply chain was in the recovery mode, having been extensively disrupted during the COVID pandemic, another crisis is looming. For example, the inert gas neon is a key ingredient in semiconductor chip making and packaging. Given that two Ukrainian companies, Ingas and Cryoin, supply from 45 to 54 percent of the world's semiconductor-grade neon and almost 90 percent of the neon supplied to the US semiconductor industry, semiconductor production will be adversely affected (Ahmad 2022).

Meanwhile, the price of the element palladium, which is used in the semiconductor packaging sector and by automakers to reduce CO_2 emissions, had skyrocketed to US$3,500 an ounce in March 2022, from US$1,900 earlier in the year. Russia accounts for 25 to 30 percent of the global supply of palladium and 35 percent of all palladium used in the United States. Should palladium be subject to prolonged sanctions on Russia, reverberations will be felt along both the electronics and the automotive GVCs.

Of the four green metals used in the production of lithium-ion batteries—lithium, nickel, manganese, and cobalt—the original equipment manufacturers are more concerned about the sustainability of the cobalt supply than about the supply of the other metals. Based on Statista data (2022) both the Philippines and Russia have similar amounts of cobalt reserves and fall within the top six country sources, after Australia, Cuba, the Democratic Republic of Congo, and Indonesia. Although the Philippines does produce nickel-cobalt mixed sulphide, the opportunity to add value and produce nickel sulphate (needed by the lithium-ion battery producers) in the Philippines has yet to be taken. Prolonged sanctions on Russian cobalt will likely increase investor interest in the Philippines.

In March 2022, more than 400 executives and investors across the life sciences industry "vowed to break ties with Russia" as a consequence of the conflict (Fidler and Pagliarulo 2022). International contract research organizations with operations in Russia are likely to curtail operations while seeking alternative options, which could include the Philippines, given the compelling investment value proposition for these organizations.

REFERENCES

Majeed Ahmad. 2022. "Ukraine War and Neon Gas Supply Disruption for Chip Manufacturing." *EDN*, March 14, 2022. https://www.edn.com/ukraine-war-and-neon-gas-supply-disruption-for-chip-manufacturing/.

Fidler, Ben, and Ned Pagliarulo. 2022. "'We Have to Make a Stand': Biotech Leaders Vow to Break Ties with Russia over Ukraine War" *Biopharmadive*, March 1, 2022. https://www.biopharmadive.com/news/biotech-business-russia-ties-ukraine-war/619611.

McKinsey Global Institute. 2020. "Risk, Resilience, and Rebalancing in Global Value Chains." McKinsey Global Institute, New York. https://www.mckinsey.com/~/media/McKinsey /Business%20Functions/Operations/Our%20Insights/Risk%20resilience%20and%20 rebalancing%20in%20global%20value%20chains/Risk-resilience-and-rebalancing-in -global-value-chains-full-report-vH.pdf.

World Bank. 2020. *World Development Report 2020: Trading for Development in the Age of Global Value Chains.* Washington, DC: World Bank.

Abbreviations

ASEAN	Association of Southeast Asian Nations
BPO	business process outsourcing
CARS	Comprehensive Automotive Resurgence Strategy
CREATE	Corporate Recovery and Tax Incentives for Enterprise
CRI	Competitiveness Reinforcement Initiative
EDSA	Epifanio de los Santos Avenue
EMS	electronics manufacturing services
FDA	US Food and Drug Administration
FDI	foreign direct investment
GDP	gross domestic product
GVC	global value chain
HLS	health and life sciences
ICT	information and communication technology
IMT	industrial, manufacturing, and transportation
IoT	Internet of Things
IT	information technology
R&D	research and development
RCEP	Regional Comprehensive Economic Partnership
TMT	technology, media, and telecommunication

1 COVID-19 and Megatrends Affecting GVCs

Following a period of hyper-globalization in 1986–2008, the fragmentation of production across borders was declining even before the COVID-19 (coronavirus) crisis (World Bank 2020). During the period of hyper-globalization, breakthrough innovation in information and communication technology, international logistics, and open trade policies allowed leading companies in sectors like electronics, automotive, and machinery to offshore parts of their production in countries with lower production costs (Antràs 2020). The global financial crisis of 2008–09, along with diminishing returns of scale for the drivers of hyper-globalization, slowed global value chain (GVC) trade. Information and communication technology innovation back then, such as broadband and computer-aided design and computer-aided manufacturing, fostered offshoring by facilitating the separation of design and manufacturing. Today, new technologies such as automation, robotics, and 3D printing are blurring the frontier between manufacturing and services, which could reinvigorate reshoring. Before COVID-19 hit in early 2020, these developments had triggered a debate about whether and how new technologies and the servicification of manufacturing might reconfigure GVCs.

The COVID-19 shock provides an opportunity for the Philippines to rethink how it participates in GVCs. Since the beginning of the COVID-19 pandemic, robust measures to contain the spread of the virus in countries central to manufacturing GVCs disrupted production and trade in other countries, including the Philippines, where foreign markets remain important both as suppliers of demand and as sources of inputs.[1] A severe and synchronized decline in exports of goods and services in 2020 led to the largest decline in the country's exports in the last four decades. Preliminary evidence points to the impact of domestic restrictions and the drop in foreign demand as the main culprits. Given how critical GVCs are to integrating the Philippines into the global economy, this book examines the impact of COVID-19 on trade by contrasting the country's trade performance before COVID-19 with insights from an analysis of high-frequency trade data since the outbreak in early 2020. This analysis is intended to inform the strategic positioning of key GVC stakeholders who are rethinking the Philippines' participation in GVCs.

THE IMPACT OF COVID-19 ON TRADE

In 2020, exports of goods and services experienced the largest decline in four decades. As shown in figure 1.1, exports experienced a severe and synchronized shock, with exports of goods (–9.7 percent) and services (–20.7 percent) declining in 2020. The combined drop in exports of goods and services was larger than in either the Asian financial crisis in 1998 (–14.7 percent) or the global financial crisis in 2008–09 (–11.8 percent). The drop in both goods and services was unlike previous episodes, where services exports proved more resilient. Goods trade fell more rapidly and recovered more swiftly than during the global financial crisis, while services trade remained depressed. The unusual nature of the COVID-19-induced recession shifted consumption toward goods and away from services requiring face-to-face interaction. The decline of goods exports in the Philippines was only slightly larger than the world's decline but much larger than the decline in all comparator countries, while the decline in services exports was similar to the world's but smaller than the decline in most peer countries, which rely more on tourism exports.

Most major goods sectors declined; service exports also performed poorly. Electronics, the country's most important export sector, contracted by 8.8 percent (figure 1.2), with almost all of the main subsectors experiencing similar declines (semiconductors, computer parts, office equipment, telecommunications) and only consumer electronics (6.9 percent) and control instrumentation (64.2 percent) experiencing positive growth in 2020. In contrast, global semiconductor exports increased 8.0 percent in 2020. Other major sectors, including transportation (–17.9 percent), agriculture (–11.6 percent), and chemicals and pharmaceuticals (–14.2 percent), also experienced significant losses. The only goods sector that experienced positive export growth was minerals (5.3 percent), largely due to the increase in the international price of copper. Tourism, which accounted for a quarter of services exports in 2019, was the hardest hit sector (–64 percent), followed by transportation (–46.4 percent). The only service sector that experienced export growth was business services (0.6 percent) (figure 1.3).

FIGURE 1.1

Growth of exports of goods and services worldwide, 2020

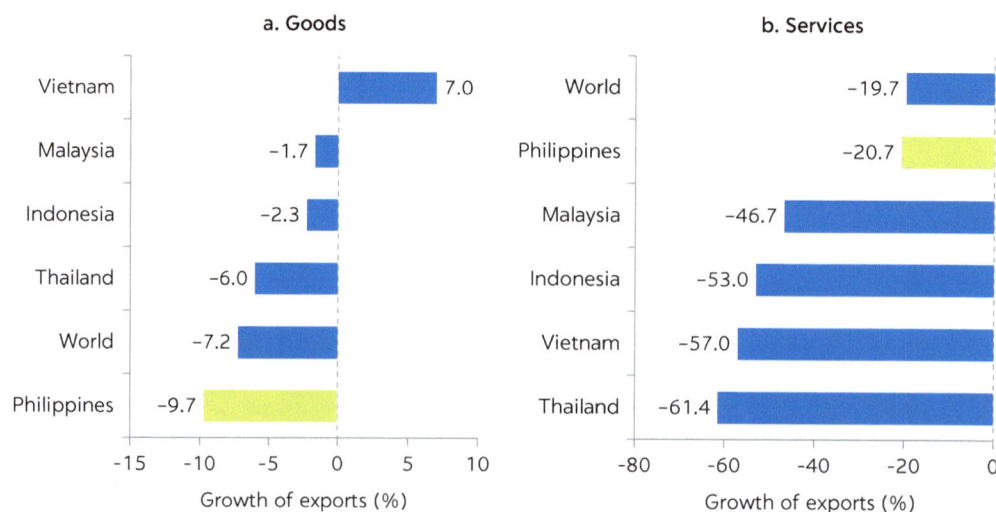

Source: World Trade Organization data.

FIGURE 1.2

Value and annual change in value of goods exports in the Philippines, 2019–20

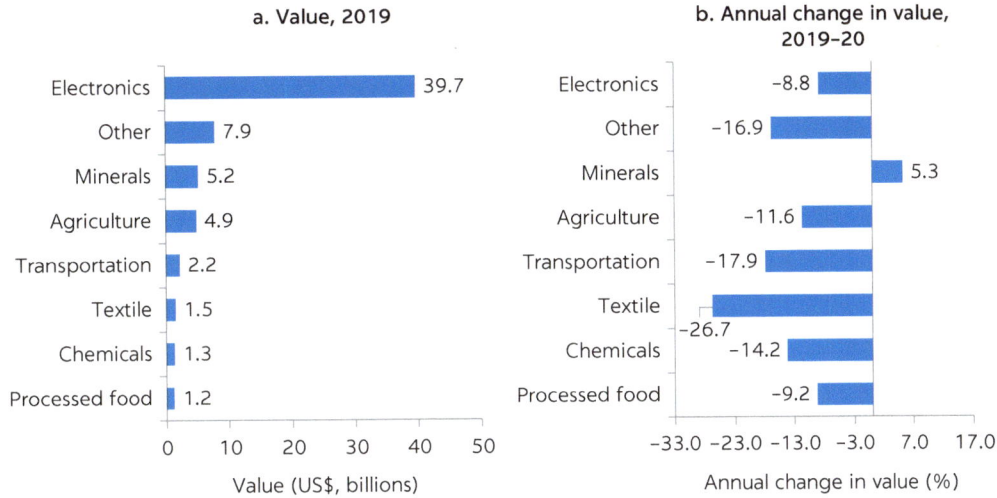

a. Value, 2019

b. Annual change in value, 2019–20

Source: Philippine Statistics Authority data.

FIGURE 1.3

Value and annual change in value of services exports in the Philippines, 2019–20

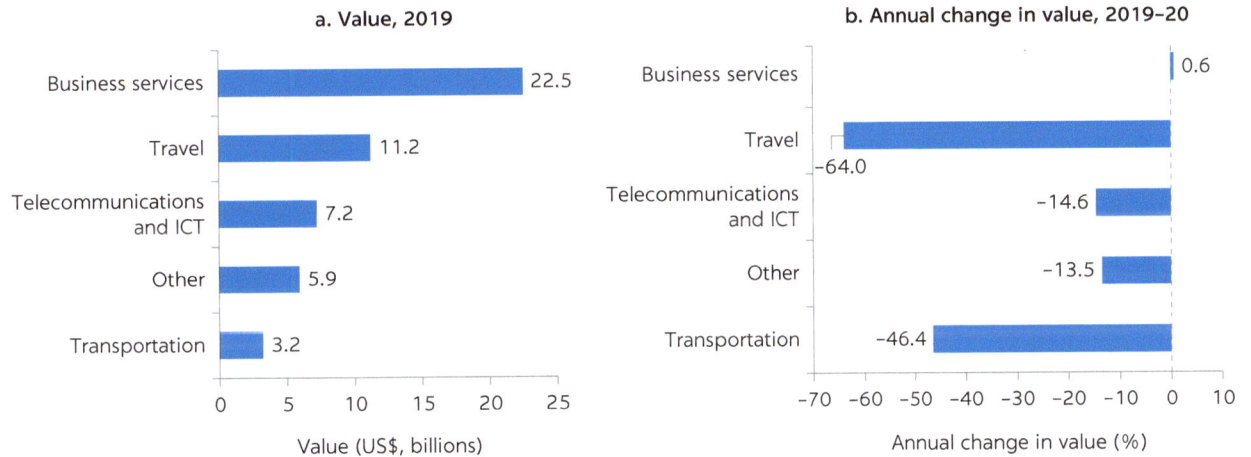

a. Value, 2019

b. Annual change in value, 2019–20

Source: Philippine Statistics Authority data.
Note: ICT = information and communication technology.

In early March 2020, the Philippines entered a highly restrictive national lockdown, with strict measures to curb infection at the beginning of the outbreak. The government first restricted international travel by banning arrivals from some regions on January 31, 2020, shortly after lockdown measures were imposed in China, Indonesia, Malaysia, and Vietnam, but before Thailand (figure 1.4). China was the only country to implement three internal measures at the beginning of the pandemic, including restraining internal movements and imposing stay-at-home orders. In March 2020, the Philippines declared a public health emergency and a state of calamity. Stringent lockdown measures were implemented, including total closure of the border on March 15, 2020, closure of workplaces and public transportation, stay-at-home requirements, and restrictions on internal movement. During the long lockdown, public transportation was curtailed, and intercity travel was prevented, disrupting

FIGURE 1.4

COVID-19 Stringency Index for the Philippines and nearby countries, 2020

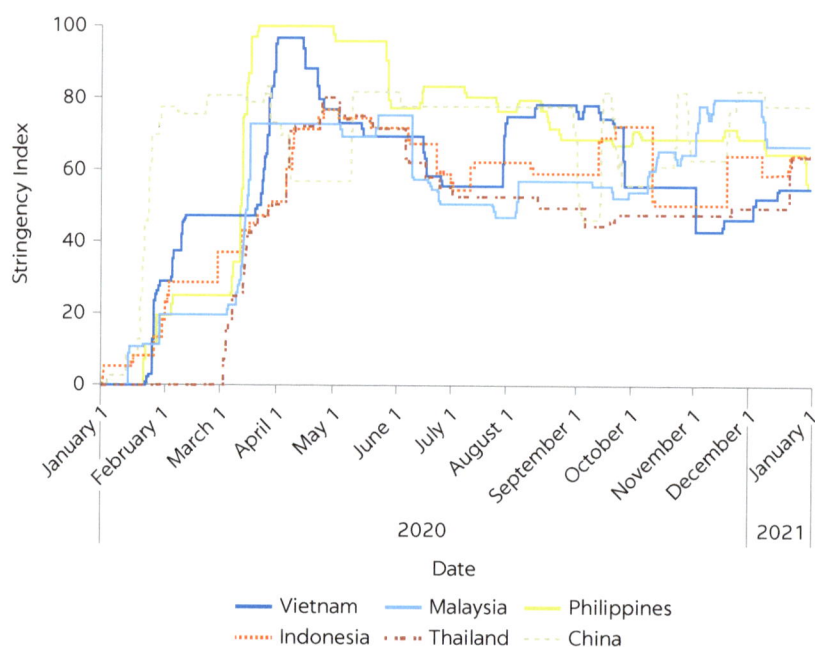

Source: Calculations based on the COVID-19 Government Responses Tracking Database; Hale et al. 2020.

many economic activities and value chains. By April, the country was feeling a sharp contraction in trade as a result of the lockdowns, with exports declining by nearly 50 percent and imports contracting by more than 65 percent (figure 1.5).

Workplace and public transportation closures, stay-at-home requirements, and restrictions on internal movement were relaxed starting on May 29, 2020. International travel controls were eased starting on July 7, 2020. While lockdown measures were reduced steadily, stay-at-home requirements and restrictions on internal movement were irregular, changing in response to the spread of the virus. The economy recovered gradually after the lockdown began to ease in June 2020. However, daily COVID-19 infections remained high after reopening, resulting in several temporary returns to strict lockdown throughout 2020 and the first half of 2021.

Electronics, the Philippines' key export sector, drove the initial contraction in trade, but also was the source of recovery in the last quarter of 2020. Across sectors, the largest decline was in electronics, with exports declining year-on-year about 80 percent in April 2020 and accounting for more than half of the year-on-year decline in exports, followed by transportation (figure 1.6). Globally, the transportation sector experienced the steepest decline: nearly 50 percent year-on-year in the second quarter of 2020. However, by September 2020, several export sectors in the Philippines began to rebound, led by electronics. The global recovery also saw a rebound in electronics products.

Foreign lockdowns had a significant impact on Philippine exports but accounted for less than a third of the decline in exports.[2] Lockdowns in the country's main trading partners were associated with a 10 percent decline in Philippine exports, on average, in the first four months after their imposition (figure 1.7). In contrast, similar analysis for Kenya showed that the introduction

FIGURE 1.5

Growth of exports in the Philippines and the world, by month, 2020

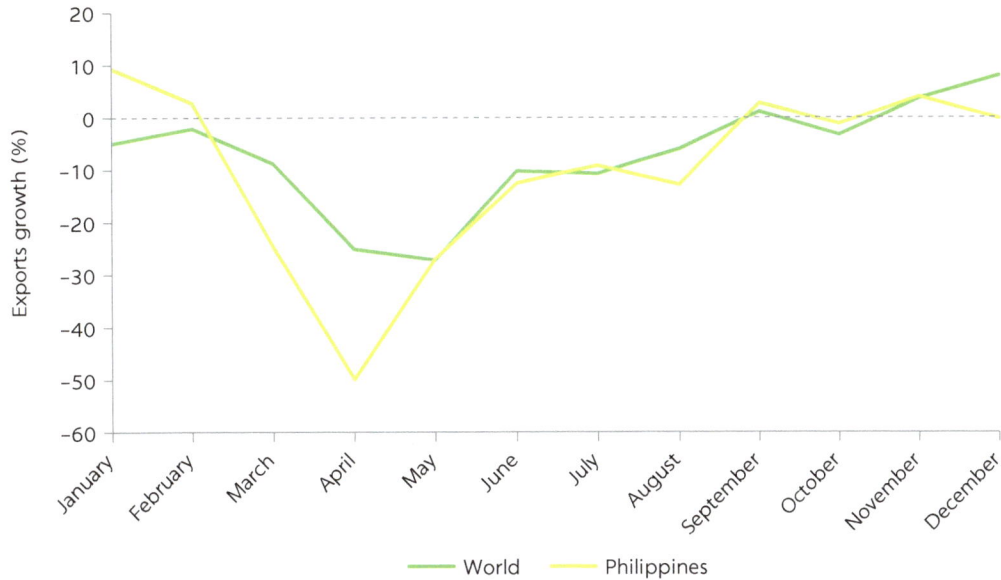

Source: Philippine Statistics Authority data.

FIGURE 1.6

Growth of exports in the Philippines, by month and sector, 2020

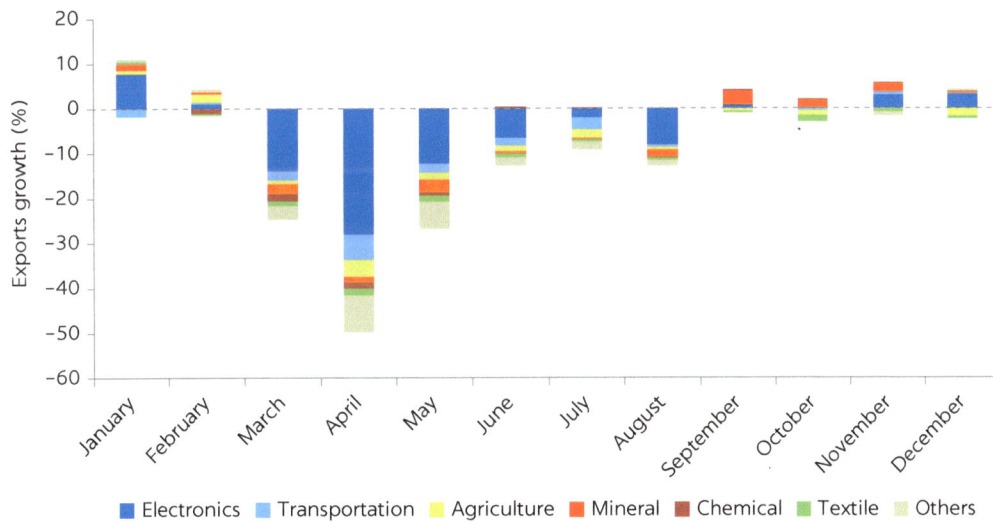

Source: Philippine Statistics Authority and World Trade Organization data.

of lockdown policies by trading partners led to an average increase in weekly exports from Kenya of 12 percent (Majune 2020). Given that Philippine exports declined by about 30 percent during that period, it appears that supply-side disruptions caused by the Philippines' own COVID-19-related restrictions were stronger than demand-side shocks. The drop in Philippine exports started one month after the imposition of lockdown policies in other countries, falling by 9.1 percent a month into the lockdown and falling consistently up to the third month, when exports contracted by 10.3 percent and then began to recover. Exports had attained pre-lockdown levels by December 2020, the eleventh month following the imposition of lockdown measures.

FIGURE 1.7

Effects of foreign lockdown policies on export trade values in the Philippines, 2020

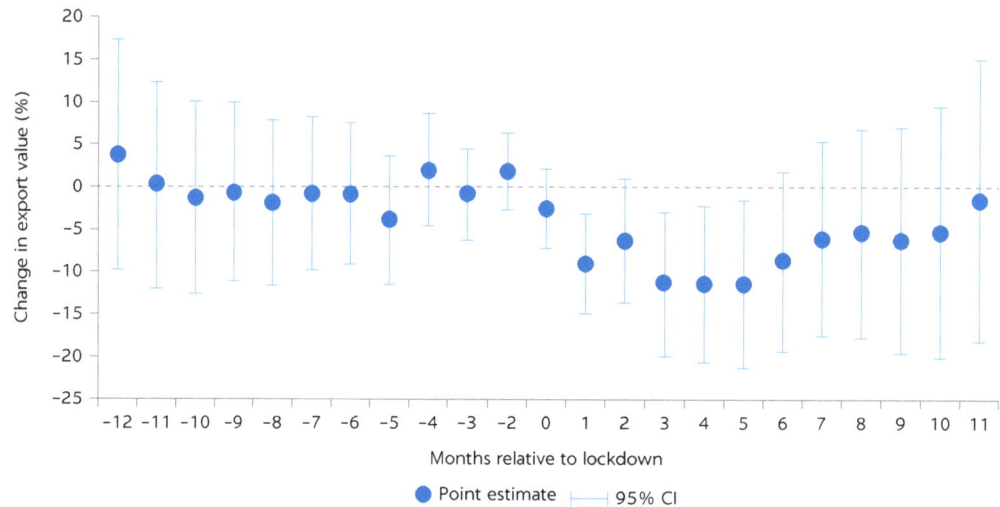

Source: Estimations from an event study based on Philippine Statistics Authority data.
Note: CI = confidence interval.

The fall in exports and imports was influenced by a decline in the trade of major products. Only semiconductors were resilient to the lockdown policies, with the share of imports and exports rising by more than 2.6 percentage points after the lockdown. Since semiconductor components and devices form the bulk of Philippine exports (at least 41 percent), their robustness after the lockdown compensated for some of the drop in other commodities, leading to a mild decline in exports compared to imports. Machinery and transportation equipment, which constitute a significant share of imports, contracted by 4.6 percentage points, explaining the massive fall in imports. Imports of consumer electronics also dropped after the Philippines' trading partners imposed lockdowns.

MEGATRENDS AFFECTING GVCs

The COVID-19 pandemic accelerated digitalization, with a profound effect on GVCs. First and foremost, digital technologies encourage GVC participation by reducing many of the barriers that firms face when attempting to join GVCs. For instance, digital platforms (such as Alibaba, Amazon, or Mercado Libre) facilitate the matching of buyers and sellers, lowering the initial fixed costs associated with GVC participation. Extending access to high-speed internet and expanding e-commerce thus have the potential to facilitate the GVC participation of firms that are relatively small or located in countries with poor infrastructure. Such firms are able to specialize in GVC segments related to the provision of services via digital technologies rather than the provision of physical goods via transportation infrastructure. These same technologies also enhance the management of inventories and logistics, improving participation in the manufacturing segments of GVCs (Antràs 2020). Furthermore, rating systems in digital platforms and openly distributed ledgers (such as blockchain) enhance verification and monitoring of firm-to-firm relationships, which can reduce information friction and open the door for countries with weak institutions to bypass a key factor limiting their participation in GVCs. Similarly, in services in which language barriers remain significant, the application of artificial intelligence, big data, and machine learning has the potential to provide much more efficient translation services. The unstoppable advance of digital technologies might provide new impetus for the continuing growth of GVC activity worldwide (Antràs 2020).

A wave of job transformations related to automation has already begun. With increased automation, work is becoming less manual and less physically demanding. The global stock of industrial robots is concentrated in specific countries and manufacturing sectors. By 2016, about 1 million industrial robots in the manufacturing sector were being used in countries specializing in innovative GVC tasks. These countries have high rates of GVC participation, a high share of manufacturing and business services in their exports, and high engagement in innovation. They include Canada, many European countries, Israel, Japan, the Republic of Korea, Singapore, and the United States (World Bank 2020). China alone used more than 260,000 robots in manufacturing production in 2019, while other countries used only 150,000 robots (figure 1.8). Nearly half of the robots were used in motor vehicle production (664,000), followed by computers and electronics (close to 400,000). Robots were used to a lesser extent to produce rubber and plastics, fabricated metals, machinery and equipment, food, and beverages (Seric and Winkler 2020).

Developments in the semiconductor industry will shape the future of these new technologies. From smartphones, computers, and pacemakers to the internet, electric vehicles, aircraft, and hypersonic weaponry, semiconductors are ubiquitous in electronic devices and the digitalization of

FIGURE 1.8

Use of industrial robots in China and other countries, by industry, 2019

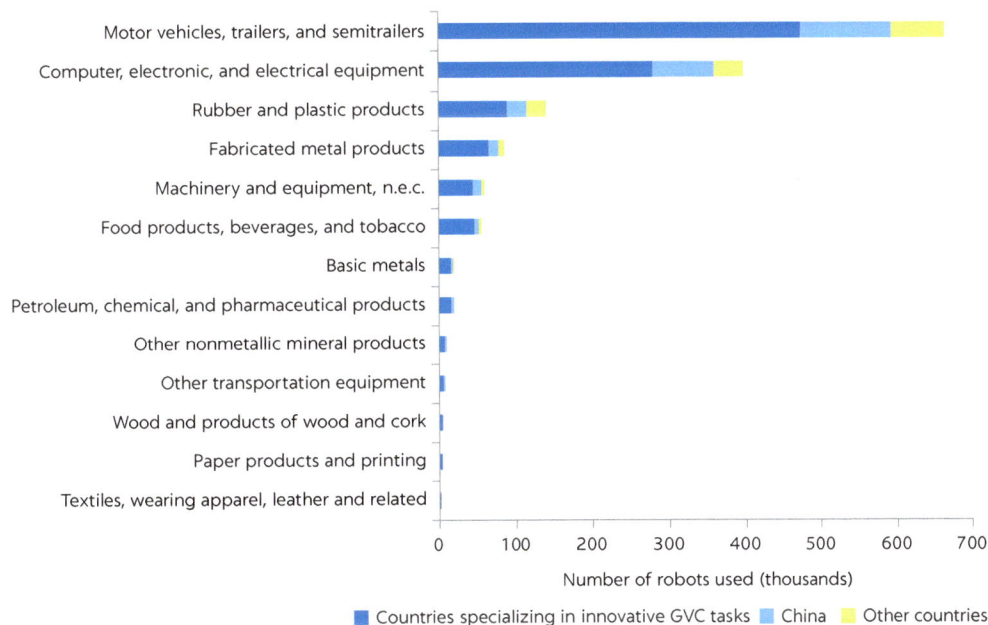

Source: Seric and Winkler 2020. Data are from the International Federation of Robotics and World Bank 2020.
Note: Number of robots refers to the operational stock of robots. The analysis is based on 59 high- and middle-income countries for which global value chain data from the TiVA database were available. GVC = global value chain; n.e.c. = not elsewhere classified.

goods and services such as global e-commerce. Demand is skyrocketing, with the industry facing numerous challenges and opportunities as emerging technologies, such as artificial intelligence, quantum computing, the Internet of Things (IoT), and 5G, all require cutting-edge semiconductor technology (Foreign Policy Insider 2021). For decades, the United States has been a leader in the semiconductor industry, controlling 48 percent (US$193 billion) of the market in terms of revenue in 2020. China has been a major importer of chips, importing US$350 billion in 2020, an increase of 14.6 percent from 2019 (Foreign Policy Insider 2021). With semiconductors at the heart of US-China strategic and technological competition, the industry continues to experience a range of protective tariff and nontariff measures that threaten the production and competitiveness of this key industry.

Semiconductors will continue to fuel geopolitical tensions between China and the United States. At its peak at the end of 2019, the United States had imposed tariffs on more than US$360 billion worth of Chinese goods, while China had retaliated, imposing import duties on US products worth about US$110 billion. Tariff and nontariff barriers can disrupt GVCs and lead to the reallocation of production nodes. The current tit-for-tat relations between China and the United States are characterized by US efforts to cut off the supply of some chips to targeted Chinese companies and to encourage the construction of advanced semiconductor factories in the United States. China has responded by threatening to sue a foreign company (Taiwan Semiconductor Manufacturing Corporation) for abiding by US rules, while at the same time pursuing the Made in China 2025 Initiative and the Guidelines to Promote National Integrated Circuit Industry Development (Foreign Policy Insider 2021). These recent developments could well lead to the disruption of key GVCs and international trade in general.

The broad application of enhanced digital technologies will affect higher-value-added services in particular. White-collar services, ranging from professional and business services to finance, engineering, and marketing activities, will become more tradable with increased digitalization (Antràs 2020); and enhanced digital technologies could make service industries the new frontier of offshoring, driven by labor cost arbitrage. High- and medium-value-added services, traditionally highly centralized, will increasingly be delivered offshore through teleworking. Teleworking opportunities are being enhanced by advanced digital communication tools, including teleconferencing, augmented reality, virtual reality, and 5G. Cloud storage and computing make it possible to perform complex tasks remotely, while improvements in translation software facilitate communication (Antràs 2020).

Services are important inputs in goods exports and can boost the competitiveness of manufacturing firms. Services are used extensively as inputs in the manufacturing process, and access to quality services is important for manufacturing performance. Lack of quality services as inputs can impede the emergence of a competitive manufacturing sector, because the performance of a firm hinges on the cost-effectiveness of the overall services environment in which the firm is operating. Transportation, telecommunications, financial, and professional services are essential to international trade.

MEGATRENDS IN GVC CLUSTERS STRATEGIC FOR THE PHILIPPINES

The Philippines' post-COVID-19 recovery could benefit from the reconfiguration of its leading export sectors in three clusters: industrial, manufacturing, and transportation (IMT); technology, media, and telecommunication (TMT); and health and life sciences (HLS). Exports from the Philippines are overly dependent on both the electronics sector and the business process management sector. Modern business and information and communication technology services combined now represent almost the same export value as electronics in terms of domestic value added. These two sectors also had the highest annualized growth rates in 2005–15. Such a concentration of exports is a source of vulnerability that calls for bold initiatives to diversify the country's export base. Manufacturing and transportation are good candidates. Most automotive exports from the Philippines consist of electronic and electrical intermediate goods, indicating some potential to diversify the country's participation in many other GVCs dealing with intermediate electronics and electrical items, including medical equipment.

The COVID-19 pandemic highlighted the need for countries to reexamine their HLS sector for opportunities to boost resilience during future pandemics. The Philippines is one of the main sources of nurses and medical staff in the world. Many of these workers returned home during the pandemic and have helped the government to implement its sanitary and medical responses to the emergency. The voice service sector is also diversifying into telemedicine, pharmacovigilance, medical transcription, clinical trial management, and patient care services and would benefit from a policy framework promoting the integration of pharmaceuticals, medical equipment, and patient care services.

Several compelling factors complement the rationale for studying the three clusters:

- *Strong foreign direct investment (FDI) demand-side dynamics based on historic trends.* Over 2018 and 2019, automotive, electronics, and information technology–enabled services were consistently top 10 performers globally, as evidenced by the number of FDI projects announced (fDi Markets 2019, 2020). In 2019, before the COVID-19 pandemic, health care had the largest increase (146 percent) in the number of projects announced per sector compared with the previous year. Aerospace is more of a niche segment, yet between 2015 and 2020 fDi Markets tracked 935 investment decisions globally, of which 8 were for the Philippines.
- *Ability to anticipate and respond to those demands.* The Philippines plays host to many of the top global investors in automotive, electronics, aerospace, business process outsourcing (BPO), and pharmaceuticals. While the existing stock of cross-border investors is impressive, efforts to increase and revitalize or upgrade the existing stock have generally plateaued over the last decade.
- *Alignment with government strategy.* The selection of the three clusters is aligned with the government's strategy and plans. The government of the Philippines has prioritized cluster-related sector development within the 2017 Inclusive Innovation Industrial Strategy and within the approved Memorandum Order no. 50 endorsing the 2020 Strategic Investments Priorities Plan, ratified in November 2020. Furthermore, pharmaceuticals were included in the plan as a priority under health care, so the selection of clusters is consistent with the government's priorities for industrial development.

- *High FDI locational mobility within the three clusters.* Locational mobility is particularly high within electronics, automotive, aerospace, and BPO; the exception is pharmaceutical investment, which tends to be more market seeking as opposed to efficiency seeking. For example, Collins Aerospace considered 32 countries across several time zones before investing in the Philippines, from where it directly supplies Airbus and Boeing with aircraft interiors.
- *Intense competition across the Asia Pacific region to attract efficiency-seeking and strategic asset–seeking investment within the clusters.* Over the last five years, Vietnam, on average, has outperformed the Philippines in attracting FDI within the three clusters by a factor of four to one. Moreover, some of the projects are very high-end research and development, including Samsung's new US$220 million global research and development hub in Hanoi, soon to employ 3,000 engineers.
- *Impact of the COVID-19 pandemic.* The profound impacts of the COVID-19 pandemic on prevailing trends in FDI, trade, and GVCs create opportunities to reconfigure GVCs. The Philippines could capitalize on these opportunities. Candid and recent feedback from investors confirms that the impact of COVID-19 has been the most disruptive they have ever encountered. However, it has also created opportunities to realign value chains and fortify links and is accelerating transformation across the three clusters. For example, the spike in demand for semiconductors will ultimately benefit semiconductor assembly and test companies in the Philippines, while the pace of change within the electric vehicle segment is unprecedented.

Industrial, manufacturing, and transportation

A series of GVC studies by Duke University in 2016 found that electronics and electrical, automotive, and aerospace GVCs could be upgraded in the Philippines (Duke University Center on Globalization, Governance, and Competitiveness 2016a, 2016b, 2016c, 2016d). The studies outline several areas that could be upgraded in IMT GVCs, including product upgrading of storage devices, entry into electrical equipment such as networking, and improvements in infrastructure. Other areas include strengthening and expanding automotive electronics and electrical products, along with backward links in common electromechanical products such as passive components, circuit boards, and electrical equipment. The studies also found challenges for the Philippines, such as competition from other Association of Southeast Asian Nations member countries, poor logistics and transportation infrastructure, and a weak position in the decision hierarchies within GVCs.

Over the last decade, the Asia Pacific region became the fastest-growing region in the world for airlines, offering opportunities for the Philippines. With almost 40 percent of airline production destined for the region, the aerospace GVC has been shifting east, creating opportunities to participate through Japanese firms. Introduction of the Boeing 787 Dreamliner was a game changer. Aircraft production broke new ground in the use of advanced weight-saving composites, the risk sharing in production development costs, and the very wide geographic spread of suppliers. The financial contribution made by Japan to development costs and the participation of Japanese firms present an opportunity for the Philippines, given the propensity of such firms to invest in the Philippines to minimize production costs.

The crisis facing the sector in 2020 was the deepest in a generation. Before the COVID-19 pandemic, Boeing halted production of its 737 MAX aircraft due to safety fears, and nearly half of all operational Boeing 737 MAX 800 airliners were grounded for similar reasons. The situation is looking more optimistic now, with Airbus increasing production in the last quarter of 2020. Furthermore, between Airbus and Boeing, more than 11,000 new aircraft have been ordered (second quarter of 2021), which will boost aircraft production and maintenance starting in mid-2022. Future aircraft configuration will likely feature less business-class capacity, and future development of the sector will be led by the push for electric and hybrid electric aircraft, defined by Airbus as "laying the groundwork for zero-emission aviation." Airbus has already developed an 80-seat hybrid electric aircraft, the E-Fan X.

The move to electric vehicles could affect countries in the IMT cluster. Mergers and acquisitions along with joint ventures have accelerated this trend over the last decade. China emerged as the top producer of electric vehicles and lithium-ion batteries. By 2019, Tesla's US$5 billion investment in Shanghai was already paying off, with sales of US$3 billion. BMW, Mercedes, and Volkswagen have all invested heavily in China. In 2018, China's largest producer of electric vehicles reached agreement with Morocco to build an electric vehicle factory—an FDI trend that will continue. By 2025, some original equipment manufacturers, such as Jaguar Land Rover, will be all electric. The rapid move to electric vehicle production, along with the outsourcing of automotive manufacturing, will be prevalent throughout the next decade. Electric vehicle sales were the least affected by the pandemic in 2020, with Tesla doubling sales in China to US$6.6 billion. Product developments such as lighter components and increased use of electronics will shift the balance of power away from original equipment manufacturers and toward firms and clusters that lead technically.

Foxconn, the world's largest electronics manufacturing service (EMS) company, is becoming a top-tier automotive supplier by developing and manufacturing entire electric vehicle systems. However, the automotive industry in the Philippines faces structural challenges. Original equipment manufacturers like Toyota will continue to struggle to achieve economies of scale in electric vehicles, despite the desire of many young Filipinos to own an electric vehicle. Countries that do not excel in conventional automotive production are very unlikely to excel in electric vehicle production. As a result, higher-value-added systems, customized design, and possibly a facility where multiple vehicle brands are assembled represent the most feasible prospects for the Philippines in this sector.[3]

The semiconductor industry is notoriously cyclical. Demand for semiconductors rose over the past decade; 2018 was a record year, with US$27.8 billion in semiconductor investment tracked globally (fDi Markets 2019). However, given the high costs of setting up (about US$10 billion) and extremely high use of energy and water, the manufacture of semiconductors is not feasible in the Philippines. Only two semiconductor manufacturing projects were tracked for the Philippines that year. Courtesy of the high stock of EMS and semiconductor investors in the Philippines, the sector accounted for 30 percent of gross domestic product and for exports valued at almost US$40 billion in 2020; at the same time, imports of electronics increased, approaching US$30 billion.

The growth of semiconductors in 5G, the IoT, and autonomous driving will continue to boost market growth. The average annual global investment of US$235 billion in expanding and strengthening 5G networks and infrastructure will have a positive downstream effect on semiconductor sales for years to come (HIS Markit 2019). The manufacturing value chain is shifting away from complex integrated circuits and silicon engineering, with companies such as Amazon, Apple, and Facebook taking advantage of fabless models[4] to design their owns chips and integrate vertically (Alam 2020). While 5G and IoT are creating opportunities for the growth of semiconductors, the manufacturing requirements for these applications differ greatly from the legacy requirements of laptops and servers. For example, a new car requires as many as 8,000 active semiconductors. Resiliency is also critical for industrial IoT applications, creating more design and test opportunities for the Philippine semiconductor industry. The global industrial IoT market is expected to grow 21.3 percent annually in 2020–28 (Quince Market Insights 2020).

The shortages of semiconductors during the first half of 2021 are resolvable. The shortages were caused by late orders for wafer fabrication by the automotive sector, which misjudged the increase in demand for electric vehicles, and higher orders for communication devices during pandemic lockdowns. A fire at a leading chip maker in Japan, Renesas, compounded concerns, given that the company controls about 35 percent of the supply of automotive chips. Semiconductor trends are generally positive, with Intel committing US$20 billion in March 2021 to build two new wafer fabrication plants in Arizona. However, for the next decade, the outsourced semiconductor assembly and test subsector will face higher risks from disruptive technologies. It is also sandwiched between foundries moving downstream and EMS companies aspiring to move upstream in GVCs. In addition to technical competence, which needs to be improved, cultural proximity and communication skills are already commendable in the Philippines, which enhances the value proposition for the design and customization of semiconductors.

The challenge for EMS companies in the Philippines is that too much business falls into the sunset category. Given the pace of technological advances, many Philippine exports will soon be obsolete. These items include hard drives, USB flash drives, and memory cards, which are being rapidly replaced by cloud storage. This challenge is occurring at a time when Vietnam is widening the gap with the Philippines in terms of greenfield EMS investment. The EMS sector may well suffer from US-China trade tensions over technologically advanced exports to the United States, in which case the Philippines may still be able to benefit from increased EMS investment.

Technology, media, and telecommunications

The key trend for BPO centers moving forward is the switch from cost saving to value addition. The next decade will also witness wider recognition in that, while the BPO sector has its own value chain, many of the BPO centers in the Philippines specialize in 9 or 10 verticals.[5] Consequently, the BPO segment contributes to the competitiveness and efficiency of the sector GVCs it is supporting. The fact that 82 percent of BPO centers and shared services centers in the Philippines serve global markets is a very positive attribute.

The next decade will see calls for reshoring, particularly from politicians in western economies. The major BPO centers in the Philippines are not fazed by this move because the economics are not feasible. Artificial intelligence–based cloud analytics and enterprise resource planning will continue to grow, while working from home is likely to outlive the COVID-19 pandemic at least to some degree.

Opinions vary on how the BPO industry will develop over the next 10 years. A 2020 Deloitte survey found that 32 percent of its clients were anticipating less outsourcing when the pandemic ends (Deloitte 2020). However, BPO centers in the Philippines will increase their share of business sourced regionally, especially from China; Hong Kong SAR, China; and Singapore, thereby reducing their dependency on the US market. The industry will spread beyond Manila, bringing new employment opportunities to other cities. The pandemic has shown that investment in telecommunications infrastructure in general—and internet bandwidth in particular—is inadequate and is compromising the ability of individuals to work from home. The Philippines hosts a group of world-class BPO centers. However, when it comes to attracting the next generation of investment in knowledge process outsourcing, the national supply of skills will have to be expanded significantly to attract higher-value-added greenfield investment that is already looking favorably at Vietnam.

Health and life sciences

Europe and the United States dominate the HLS sector, accounting for 78 percent of the global export market. China's share of the personal protective equipment industry is high, at 22 percent, and rises to more than 50 percent for specific items such as masks, protective goggles, and protective gowns. According to Baker McKenzie (2020),

> Healthcare and Life Sciences companies now face increased complexity in managing their supply chains, given the host of legal and regulatory measures arising out of COVID-19. Companies will now be pushed to work even harder as manufacturers evaluate their entire supply chain amid heightened awareness of potential shortages and disruptions that may be caused by the pandemic. These [disruptions] would relate to active pharmaceutical ingredients, finished-dose forms, and any components that are affected by special regulation or government intervention. As companies plan ahead, sustainability, market access, and IP [intellectual property] risks will be key concerns for HLS supply chains.

In contrast, global pharmaceutical innovation is dominated by China, the European Union, and the United States (figure 1.9). In 2020, these three entities, along with Japan and the Republic of Korea (all of them important trading partners of the Philippines) published the greatest number of patents in the pharmaceutical industry.

FIGURE 1.9

Patents published in the pharmaceutical industry, by country, 2020

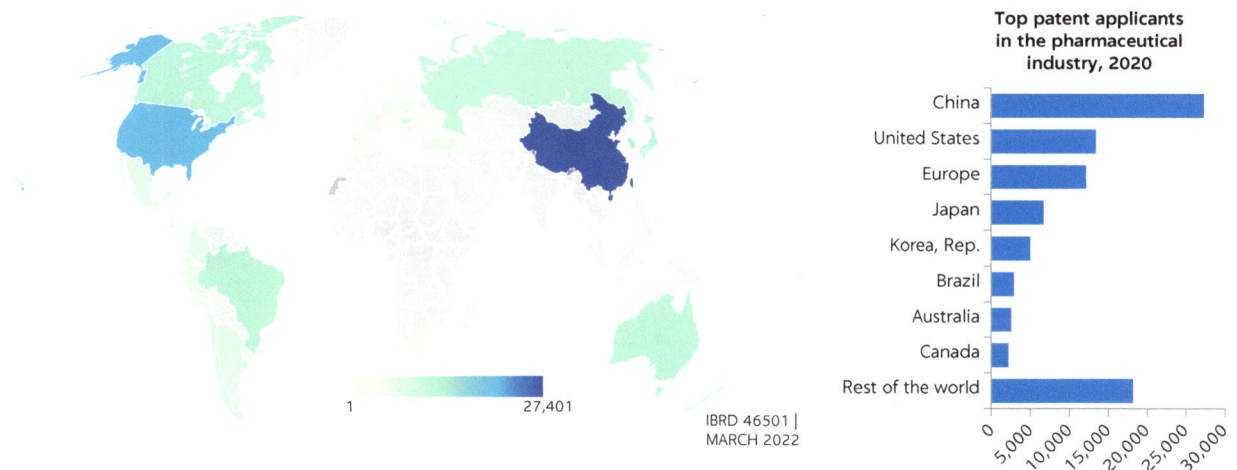

Source: World Bank, based on World Intellectual Property Organization data.

The HLS cluster is facing challenges such as sustainability, market access, and intellectual property risks that present opportunities for the Philippines. As pharmaceuticals, medical devices, and health care services become more integrated and the management of information becomes as important as the management of products,[6] development of the IMT and TMT clusters could facilitate the emergence of an HLS cluster in the Philippines, with the IMT cluster (through electronic components) reaching the medical devices sector, the TMT cluster (through health care information technology services) reaching the health care service sector, and the pharma sector attracting lead multinational corporations, while promoting networks of domestic suppliers.

The pharmaceutical GVC is quite opaque, which has exacerbated the disruptions triggered by the COVID-19 pandemic. The COVID-19 stress experienced by pharmaceutical GVCs at the height of the health crisis illustrates the risks posed by relying too heavily on China and India. A clear trend during the last decade was increased merger and acquisition activity in the sector, leading to increased market concentration and dominance by a few big players. The last decade also witnessed a sustained increase in global pharmaceutical investment. The value of biotechnology global investment projects announced increased from about US$3.1 billion in 2014 to more than US$7.2 billion in 2018 (fDi Markets 2019).

Over the next decade, more emphasis will be placed on research and discovery, along with clinical developments. Multinational corporations will continue manufacturing medicines faster and more cost-effectively, while smaller, innovative, more agile companies will take their products to market. Contract research organization activity will increase, as will the big data and analytical needs of the health care sector. These areas offer the Philippines additional opportunities for growth of the BPO and information technology outsourcing sectors. But the lack of a life sciences and biotechnology ecosystem means that, for the next decade, the country is poorly placed to capitalize on the growth of the biopharmaceutical sector. Neither pharmaceutical multinational corporations nor large indigenous companies in the Philippines tend to export, resulting in pharmaceutical imports being 33 times greater than exports in 2019.[7] The Philippines needs to address this imbalance; technical assistance and expertise would help to invigorate the embryonic life sciences sector. Success in this area would turn the COVID-19 crisis into an opportunity, with the post-COVID-19 recovery benefiting from the reconfiguration of the country's leading export sectors in the three clusters.

NOTES

1. In late March 2020, one month after COVID-19 was declared a pandemic, China, Germany, Japan, the Republic of Korea, and the United States, five countries central to manufacturing GVCs across the world, had 42 percent of cases worldwide (Baldwin and Weder di Mauro 2020).

2. An event-study methodology following Majune (2020) was employed to investigate the impact of lockdown policies on the Philippines' import and export trade. Monthly product-country data are for January 2019 to December 2020. Data for lockdown measures were obtained from the COVID-19 Government Responses Tracking Database compiled by Blavatnik School of Government of the University of Oxford (Hale et al. 2020).

3. Toyota Aisin manufactures traditional transmissions (five-speed gearboxes) in the Philippines, of which 95 percent are exported, mainly to Thailand. For companies like this

to decide to manufacture electric vehicle transmission in the Philippines, improvements are essential in a few areas: skills development, ability to source the lightweight alloy casings and key electronic components (for example, hydrostatic brake actuators, speed sensors, and oil cooler and electric oil pumps), research and development competencies in composites, lithium-ion battery technology, and a move from one-speed transmissions to two-speed transmissions. Such improvements would help to place the Philippines on the radar of electric vehicle companies and suppliers.

4. The design and sale of semiconductors while outsourcing their fabrication.
5. A vertical BPO domain provides various functional services in a limited number of industry domains. Health care, financial services, manufacturing, and retail are examples of vertical BPO domains.
6. See www.pwc.com/pharma2020.
7. United Laboratories, a Filipino company, is the largest pharmaceutical company in Southeast Asia. It sets up local factories to supply different markets directly.

REFERENCES

Alam, Syed. 2020. "The Future of Semiconductor Manufacturing." *Electronic Times,* November 6, 2020.

Antràs, Pol. 2020. "De-Globalization? Global Value Chains in the Post-Covid-19 Age." NBER Working Paper 28115, National Bureau of Economic Research, Cambridge, MA.

Baker McKenzie. 2020. "Supply Chains Reimagined: Recovery and Renewal in Asia Pacific and Beyond." Baker McKenzie, Chicago, IL.

Baldwin, Richard, and Beatrice Weder di Mauro. 2020. *Economics in the Time of COVID-19.* London: Centre for Economic Policy Research.

Deloitte. 2020. *How Much Disruption? Deloitte Global 2020 Global Outsourcing Survey.* London: Deloitte.

Duke University Center on Globalization, Governance, and Competitiveness. 2016a. "The Philippines in the Aerospace Global Value Chain." Duke University, Durham, NC.

Duke University Center on Globalization, Governance, and Competitiveness. 2016b. "The Philippines in the Automotive Global Value Chain." Duke University, Durham, NC.

Duke University Center on Globalization, Governance, and Competitiveness. 2016c. "The Philippines in the Electronics and Electrical Global Value Chain." Duke University, Durham, NC.

Duke University Center on Globalization, Governance, and Competitiveness. 2016d. "The Philippines Upgrading in the Manufacturing Global Value Chain." Duke University, Durham, NC.

European Patent Office. 2020. "Patent Index 2020." European Patent Office, Munich. https://epo.org/patent-index2020.

fDi Markets. 2019. *fDi Report 2019 Global Greenfield Investment Trends.* London: Financial Times.

fDi Markets. 2020. *fDi Report 2020 Global Greenfield Investment Trends.* London: Financial Times.

Foreign Policy Insider. 2021. *Semiconductors and the U.S.-China Innovation Race: Geopolitics of the Supply Chain and the Central Role of Taiwan.* Special report by FP Analytics, Washington, DC, February 16, 2021. https://foreignpolicy.com/2021/02/16/semiconductors-us-china-taiwan-technology-innovation-competition/.

Hale, Thomas, Anna Petherick, Toby Phillips, and Samuel Webster. 2020. "Variation in Government Responses to COVID-19." Working Paper version 6, Blavatnik School of Government, Oxford.

HIS Markit. 2019. "The 5G Economy: How 5G Will Contribute to the Global Economy." HIS Markit, London.

Majune, Socrates. 2020. "The Effect of Lockdown Policies on International Trade Flows from Developing Countries: Event Study Evidence from Kenya." World Trade Organization, Geneva. https://www.wto.org/english/news_e/news20_e/rese_15dec20_e.pdf.

Quince Market Insights. 2020. "Industrial Internet of Things (IoT) Market Is Anticipated to Grow at a CAGR of 21.3% during 2020 to 2028." Quince Market Insights, Pune, India. https://www.quincemarketinsights.com/industry-analysis/industrial-internet-of -things-iiot-market.

Seric, Adnan, and Deborah Winkler. 2020. "COVID-19 Could Spur Automation and Reverse Globalisation—to Some Extent." *VOXEU/CEPR* (blog), April 28, 2020.

World Bank. 2020. *World Development Report 2020: Trading for Development in the Age of Global Value Chains.* Washington, DC: World Bank.

2 Rethinking GVC Participation in the Philippines

Trade, investment, technology, and geopolitical trends that predate the pandemic will have profound implications for the Philippines' participation in global value chains (GVCs). These trends include the rise of automation and artificial intelligence, which will erode traditional comparative advantages based on low wages, and the increasing use of services in manufacturing, which will fuel demand for highly skilled workers. Another important trend is enhanced digitalization of supply chains, which will necessitate the rapid adoption of new technologies. Significant opportunities will arise for specific GVC clusters brought about by the switch from combustion engine cars to electric vehicles and the regionalization of the aeronautics value chain. The increase in demand for semiconductors from the expansion of 5G, the Internet of Things, and data-driven integrated health care systems will provide other opportunities. As illustrated in figure 2.1, robotization will have a substantial impact on the process of GVC reconfiguration in the Philippines after COVID-19.

The Philippines is one of many countries that have climbed the GVC ladder in recent decades. Over the period 1990–2015, the following countries moved from limited manufacturing GVCs into advanced manufacturing and services GVCs: China, the Czech Republic, Estonia, India, Lithuania, the Philippines, Poland, Portugal, Romania, Thailand, and Turkey (World Bank 2020b). For advanced manufacturing GVCs, the process of importing to export increases the dependence on upstream inputs and the exposure to upstream risks. Upstream risks refer to supply shocks on the sourcing side that result from unforeseen events or bottlenecks taking place along the value chain of upstream suppliers. These risks are testing the resilience of GVCs in the Philippines.

THE PHILIPPINES' GVC PARTICIPATION

The Philippines' backward GVC participation in the industrial, manufacturing, and transportation (IMT) cluster has improved visibly since 2010. After weak performance from the mid-2000s to 2010, the IMT cluster recovered and is participating increasingly in GVCs (figure 2.2). Backward participation grew faster than forward participation and was greater in magnitude,

Imports of industrial robots in the Philippines, 2019–20

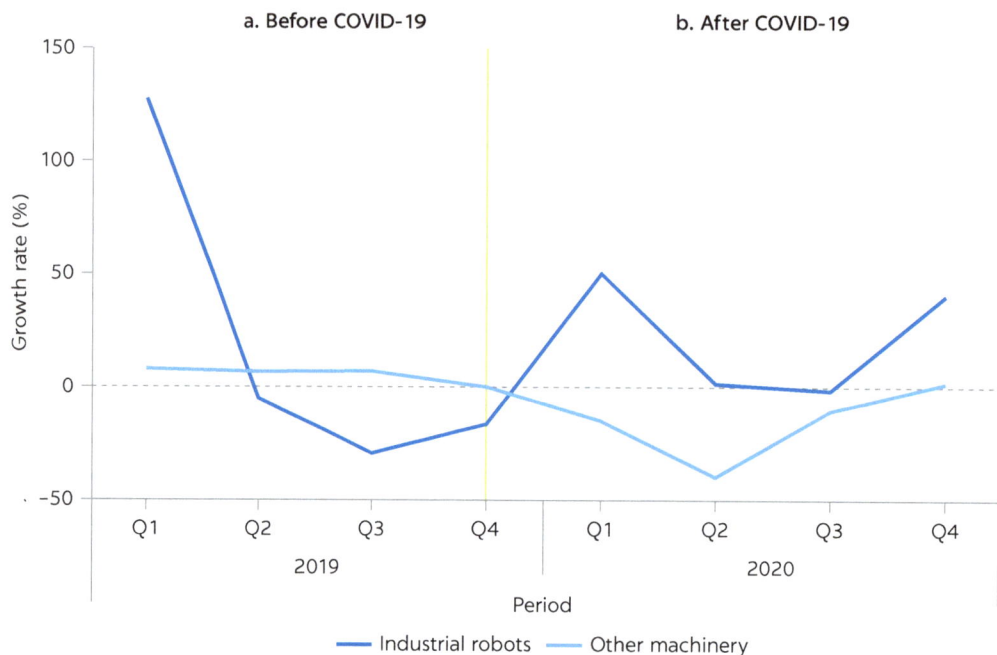

Source: Based on Philippine Statistics Authority data.

suggesting that the Philippines is taking on progressively more advanced tasks in GVCs. The improvements in backward GVC activities in the machinery and electrical equipment sectors are particularly remarkable. Nevertheless, the Philippines is trailing behind its regional peers, especially in the transportation equipment sector.

The Philippines' participation in the technology, media, and telecommunication (TMT) cluster did not change much from 2007 to 2017. Both forward and backward GVC activities were small and comparable in size (figure 2.3). The Philippines has a relatively higher proportion of graduates in the information and communication technology field than its regional peers, but fewer GVC activities. Nevertheless, the Philippines managed to triple the number of mobile internet users to 73 million in 2010–20 (World Bank 2020a). Upgrading digital infrastructure, harnessing market opportunities, improving the country's logistics, and improving the business environment would expand the sector's contribution to the economy (World Bank 2020a). Moreover, addressing the digital divide by improving connectivity would create significant economic and social potential. Vietnam is a good example to emulate in this regard.

The Philippines' GVC participation in the health and life sciences (HLS) cluster is declining slowly, and backward participation is relatively higher than forward participation. Compared to the sector's value added, GVC participation is quite low (figure 2.4). Compared to its regional peers, the Philippines is the lowest performer. However, this ranking may not be a discouraging sign. Endowment, geography, market size, and institutions are the crucial elements for transitioning to more sophisticated participation in GVCs (World Bank 2020b). Given the country's considerable similarities to its peers in several dimensions, addressing major constraints in the HLS sector could unleash the untapped potential to succeed in this particular area. Reaping this low-hanging fruit would open further

FIGURE 2.2

GVC participation in the industrial, manufacturing, and transportation sector in select countries, 2007–17

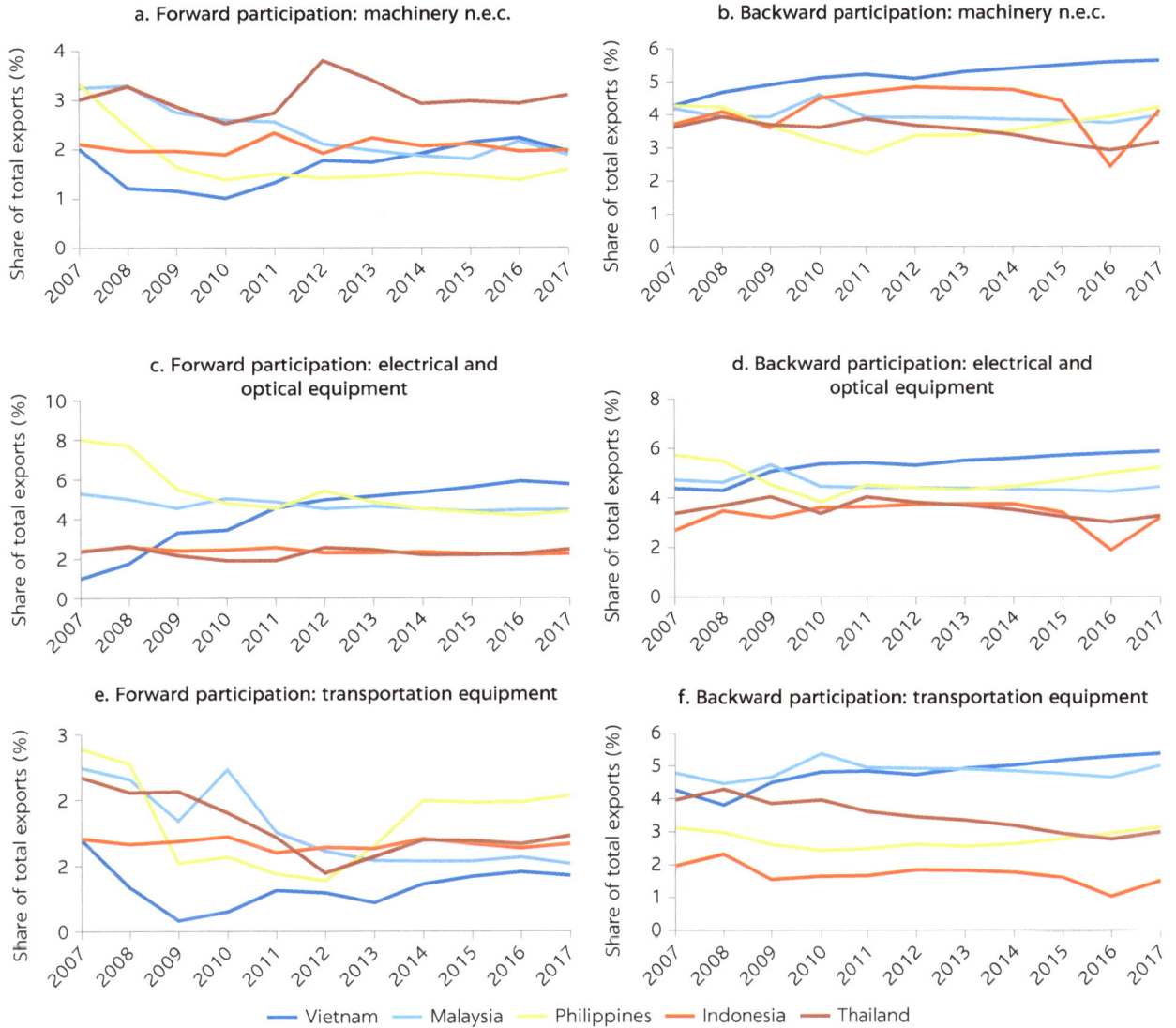

a. Forward participation: machinery n.e.c.

b. Backward participation: machinery n.e.c.

c. Forward participation: electrical and optical equipment

d. Backward participation: electrical and optical equipment

e. Forward participation: transportation equipment

f. Backward participation: transportation equipment

— Vietnam — Malaysia — Philippines — Indonesia — Thailand

Source: Computations based on the Asian Development Bank (ADB) Multiregional Input-Output (MRIO) database.

FIGURE 2.3

GVC participation in the telecommunications sector in select countries, 2007–17

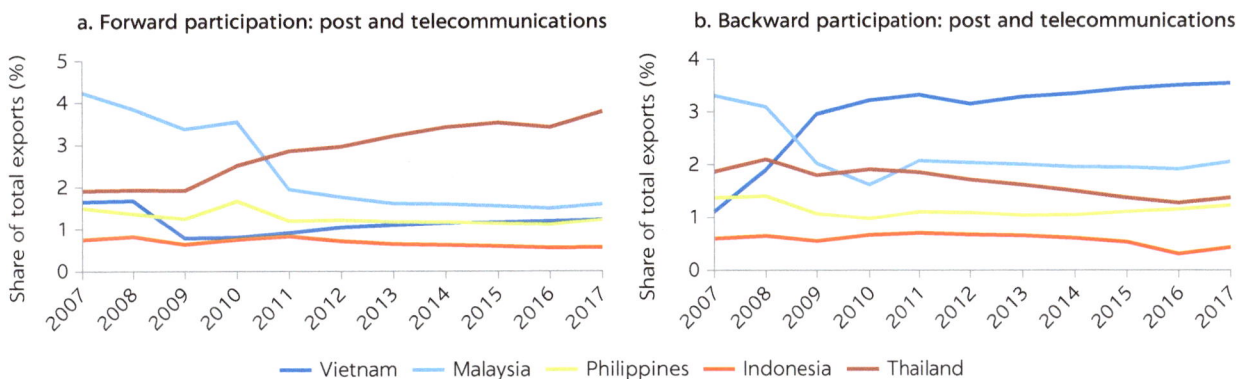

a. Forward participation: post and telecommunications

b. Backward participation: post and telecommunications

— Vietnam — Malaysia — Philippines — Indonesia — Thailand

Source: Computations based on the Asian Development Bank (ADB) Multiregional Input-Output (MRIO) database.

FIGURE 2.4

GVC participation in the health and life sciences sector in select countries, 2007–17

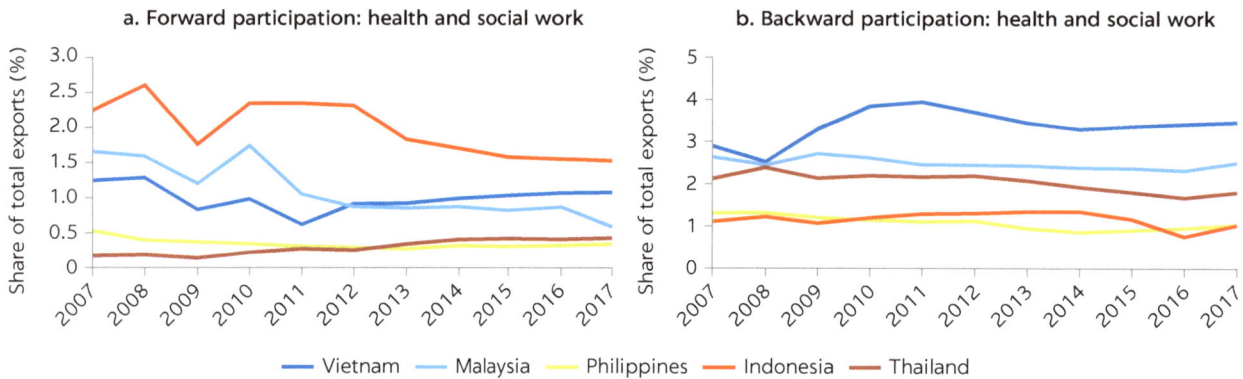

a. Forward participation: health and social work

b. Backward participation: health and social work

Vietnam — Malaysia — Philippines — Indonesia — Thailand

Source: Computations based on the Asian Development Bank (ADB) Multiregional Input-Output (MRIO) database.

opportunities to take on more advanced GVC activities. The chemical industry, which is closely related to the pharmaceutical industry, is following a similar trend.

The COVID-19 crisis offers public and private stakeholders an opportunity to rethink the Philippines' participation in strategic GVC clusters. Beyond COVID-19, China's economic rebalancing (and ongoing trade war with the United States) provides a window of opportunity for the Philippines. China's labor costs are rising, growing more than sixfold from 2000 to 2012 and overtaking agglomeration economies in key urban centers. Several electronics firms currently in China may be looking for alternative production facilities in the coming years.

GVCs offer small and medium enterprises an opportunity to learn, upgrade, and improve their competitiveness. Although eight Philippine companies are among the world's largest listed firms, the private sector is still dominated by a few large conglomerates that, either by design or by chance, have made some sectors less open than they should be. In addition to policies that keep investment fully open, transparent, and fair, an overarching policy goal is needed to address the problem of the "missing middle" and bridge the huge inequality gap. This effort would practically and pragmatically accelerate the growth and internationalization of small and medium enterprises in the Philippines. Participation in GVCs can bring considerable benefits to domestic firms because they can learn from multinational corporations through investment, partnerships, or trade, as documented in Qiang, Liu, and Steenbergen (2021). Such knowledge can help firms to raise domestic productivity, to obtain the production capabilities and foreign knowledge they need to compete directly in international markets, and to upgrade their roles in GVCs.

PHILIPPINE TRADE PERFORMANCE BEFORE COVID-19

The megatrends under way have profound implications for the Philippines. In contrast to peer countries that have generated a strong base of manufacturing exports, services in the Philippines accounted for only 23 percent of value added in manufacturing exports in 2016, a share roughly unchanged since 2005 (22 percent). The share in the Philippines is lower than in China, Malaysia, and Thailand and lower than the average shares in the Association of Southeast

Asian Nations and the Organisation for Economic Co-operation and Development (figure 2.5).

Furthermore, the contribution of modern services is low, with links to traditional rather than modern services. Distribution services, such as wholesale and retail activities, are the most important services inputs for manufacturing production in the Philippines. The links between financial services and manufacturing are particularly weak, and access to finance is a serious constraint in the Philippines. In 2015, financial services represented only about 3 percent of total services inputs in manufacturing. The share of investment that is financed through firms' own funds—or the ratio of collateral to total loans—is very high, suggesting that firms find it difficult to obtain finance. The Philippines is a service economy and a lead exporter of services, but efficient links between services and other sectors are lacking. With its remarkable human assets, the country has solid fundamentals and capacity to leapfrog into the Fourth Industrial Revolution. To do so, it needs to increase the share of innovation and services in exports and take advantage of the opportunity to link its services and manufacturing sectors.

The contribution of trade to Philippine gross domestic product declined steadily during the last two decades. Trade openness declined by more than 40 points of gross domestic product over the past 20 years, putting the country at odds with its peers (figure 2.6). Export growth slowed significantly, especially after the global financial crisis in 2008–09, averaging 4 percent in 2000–08 and 2.5 percent in 2008–19 (figure 2.7). The domestic economy grew faster during this period (4.6 percent in 2000–08 and 6.4 percent in 2008–19), as the country increasingly relied on investment and domestic consumption to fuel growth.

Services became almost as important as goods in generating exports before the COVID-19 pandemic. While goods still represent 60 percent of total exports, this share declined continuously during the period, and export growth was driven primarily by services. During the last decade, the export growth of manufactured goods stood at 4.7 percent, compared to double-digit growth of services (12.9 percent). Electronics—the main source of manufactured exports for

FIGURE 2.5

Share of services value added in manufacturing and electronics exports in select countries

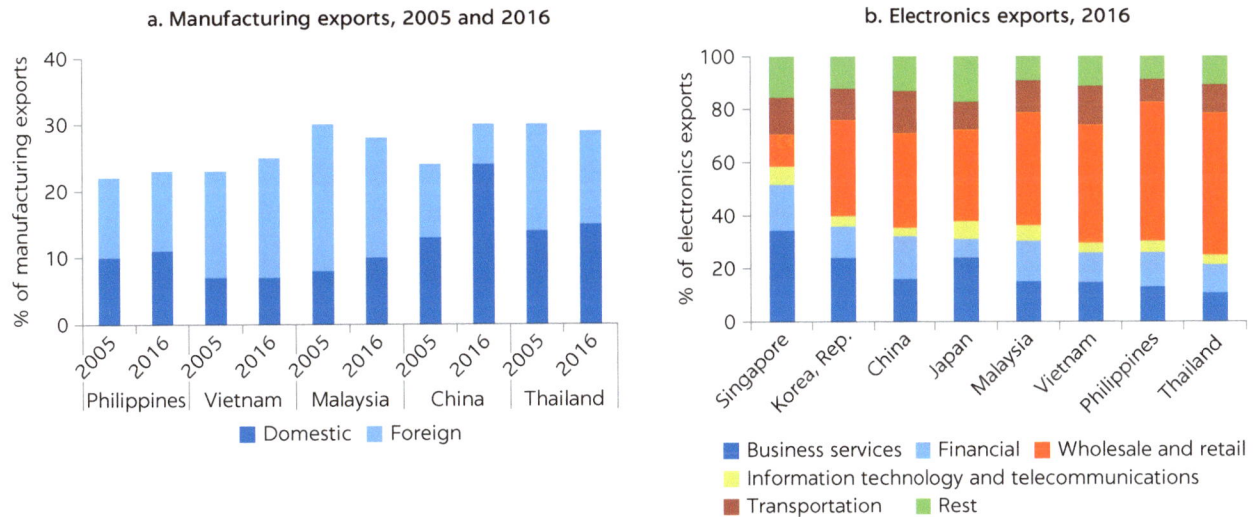

a. Manufacturing exports, 2005 and 2016

b. Electronics exports, 2016

Source: Based on Organisation for Economic Co-operation and Development (OECD) Trade in Value Added (TiVA) data.

FIGURE 2.6
Share of trade in GDP in select countries, 1990–2019

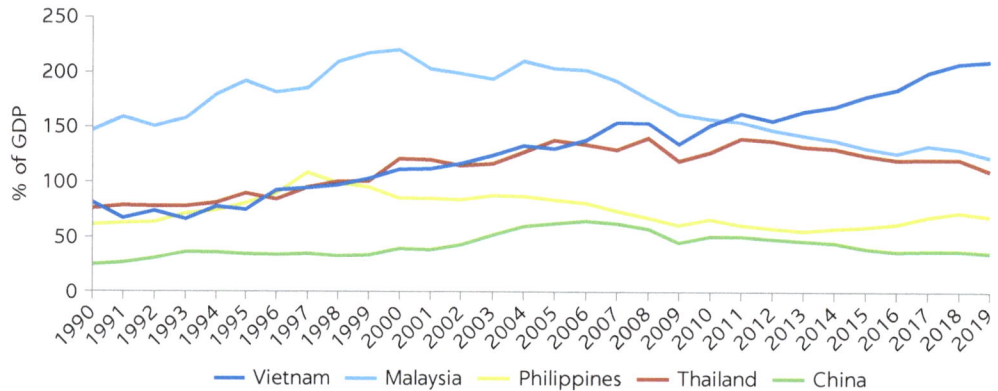

Source: World Bank, World Development Indicators data.

FIGURE 2.7
Share of exports in GDP in the Philippines, 2000–19

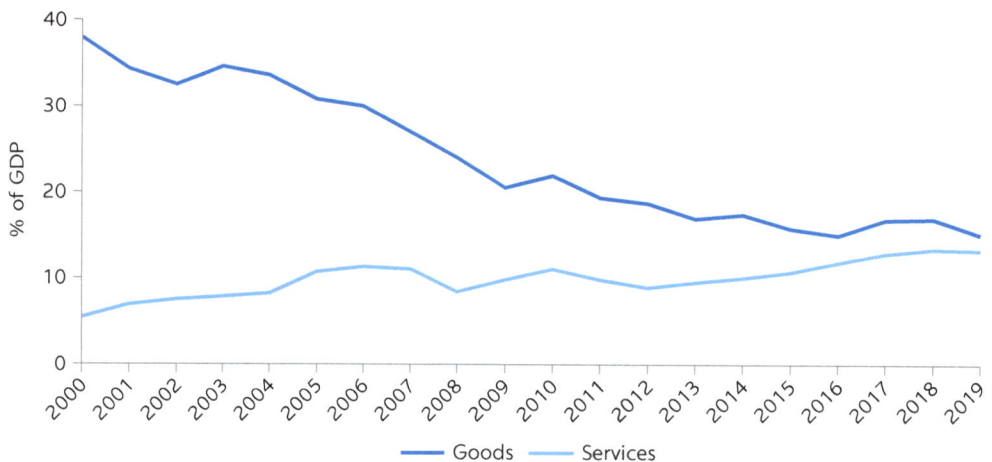

Source: Philippine Statistics Authority data.

the Philippines—stagnated at less than 2 percent growth, while the Philippines' competitors in the sector grew very fast (25.5 percent in Vietnam and 23.1 percent in China). The Philippines has missed several opportunities in its main field of exports.

Although textiles and agricultural exports traditionally dominated the export basket, electronics has been the main export sector for the last two decades. From 2008 to 2019, the Philippines moved away from textiles (dropping from 4.1 percent to 1.5 percent of exports) to electronics and electrical products (growing from 54.3 percent to 57.0 percent of exports) (table 2.1). This move was due largely to the new multilateral trade rules and the phasing out of old quotas and other quantitative or tariff restrictions on textiles and apparel.

China became one of the most important destinations for exports over the last decade, to the detriment of the United States. The share of exports going to China increased from 1.7 percent in 2000 to 13.8 percent in 2019, while the share going to Hong Kong SAR, China, increased from 5.0 percent to 13.6 percent during the same period. Conversely, the US share of exports declined from

TABLE 2.1 Exports of the Philippines, by sector, 2000–19

SECTOR	VALUE (US$, MILLIONS)			SHARE OF TOTAL (%)			ANNUAL GROWTH (%)	
	2000	2008	2019	2000	2008	2019	2000–08	2008–19
Electronic products	21,723	23,581	32,391	68.4	54.3	57.0	1.0	2.9
Semiconductors	15,228	16,090	22,393	47.9	37.1	39.4	0.7	3.1
Electronic data processing	4,909	5,134	4,067	15.5	11.8	7.2	0.6	−2.1
Office equipment	80	308	1,640	0.3	0.7	2.9	18.4	16.4
Consumer electronics	462	473	1,029	1.5	1.1	1.8	0.3	7.3
Telecommunication	207	302	625	0.7	0.7	1.1	4.8	6.8
Automotive electronics	353	809	152	1.1	1.9	0.3	10.9	−14.1
Other	483	465	2,485	1.5	1.1	4.4	−0.5	16.5
Agricultural products	1,327	2,538	4,749	4.2	5.8	8.4	8.4	5.9
Processed food and beverages	158	552	780	0.5	1.3	1.4	16.9	3.2
Machinery and transportation equipment	1,025	2,551	4,911	3.2	5.9	8.6	12.1	6.1
Ignition wiring sets	562	875	2,216	1.8	2.0	3.9	5.7	8.8
Metals	459	1,833	2,930	1.4	4.2	5.2	18.9	4.4
Copper cathodes	227	1,271	1,217	0.7	2.9	2.1	24.0	−0.4
Chemicals	248	1,058	1,269	0.8	2.4	2.2	19.9	1.7
Textiles and apparel	2,340	1,771	834	7.4	4.1	1.5	−3.4	−6.6
Other	3,887	7,982	7,905	12.2	18.4	13.9	9.4	−0.1
Total	**31,774**	**43,394**	**56,789**	**100**	**100**	**100**	**4.0**	**−2.5**

Source: Philippine Statistics Authority data.

29.5 percent in 2000 to 16.3 percent in 2019 (table 2.2). China has become the main manufacturing hub for electronics and the largest consumer of semiconductors and other electronics intermediates exported by the Philippines.

Philippine exports are among the most concentrated (in terms of products and firms) in the region. The Philippines' reliance on semiconductor exports is among the highest in the world, accounting for a third of the country's total exports (figure 2.8). Furthermore, only a handful of firms account for almost three-quarters of semiconductor exports (figure 2.9). If one of these firms decides to restructure and leave the Philippines, this decision will have a big impact on total exports (for example, Intel's exit in 1998). Semiconductors are also a cyclical sector, which exposes the Philippines to international shocks.

The remarkable expansion of services exports was driven mainly by business and computer services. Services exports increased tenfold over the last two decades due to the increase in exports of business process outsourcing (BPO) and computer services. Tourism, which had traditionally been the most important services export, grew slowly during much of the period, although it has been growing as fast as the BPO sector since 2016. Services exports are more western focused (the United States accounts for 24 percent of BPO demand, and the European Union accounts for 33 percent); unlike goods exports, they do not depend on East Asia. By contrast, a large share of exports of post and telecommunications and transportation and storage is consumed in Association of Southeast Asian Nations member countries (22 percent and 23 percent, respectively) and East Asia (23 percent and 30 percent, respectively).

TABLE 2.2 **Exports of the Philippines, by destination, 2000–19**

DESTINATION	VALUE (US$, MILLIONS)			SHARE TOTAL (%)			ANNUAL GROWTH (%)	
	2000	2008	2019	2000	2008	2019	2000–08	2008–19
United States	11,240	8,146	11,560	29.5	16.6	16.3	−3.9	3.2
Japan	5,606	7,706	10,670	14.7	15.7	15.1	4.1	3.0
China	663	5,469	9,814	1.7	11.1	13.8	30.2	5.5
Hong Kong SAR, China	1,907	4,987	9,625	5.0	10.2	13.6	12.8	6.2
Singapore	3,124	2,607	3,832	8.2	5.3	5.4	−2.2	3.6
Korea, Rep.	1,173	2,523	3,241	3.1	5.1	4.6	10.0	2.3
Thailand	1,206	1,509	2,972	3.2	3.1	4.2	2.8	6.4
Germany	1,329	2,440	2,723	3.5	5.0	3.8	7.9	1.0
Netherlands	2,982	3,708	2,266	7.8	7.6	3.2	2.8	−4.4
Taiwan, China	2,861	1,862	2,253	7.5	3.8	3.2	−5.2	1.7
Malaysia	1,372	1,946	1,825	3.6	4.0	2.6	4.5	−0.6
Vietnam	75	385	1,270	0.2	0.8	1.8	22.8	11.5
Indonesia	183	603	829	0.5	1.2	1.2	16.0	2.9
France	295	259	802	0.8	0.5	1.1	−1.6	10.8
Mexico	285	174	672	0.7	0.4	0.9	−6.0	13.1
Other	3,771	4,754	6,563	10	10	9	2.9	3.0
Total	**38,072**	**49,078**	**70,917**	**100**	**100**	**100**	**3.2**	**3.4**

Source: Philippine Statistics Authority data.

FIGURE 2.8

Share of semiconductor exports in total exports in select economies, 2019

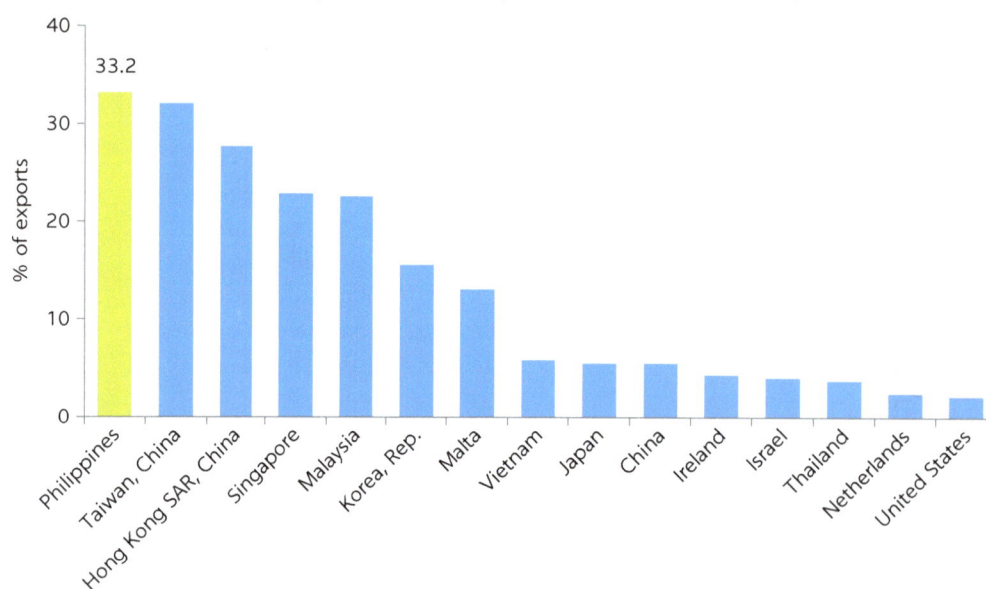

Source: United Nations Comtrade data.

FIGURE 2.9

FIGURE 2.9

Share of top six firms in semiconductor exports in the Philippines, 2019

Semiconductor exports by firm (% total)

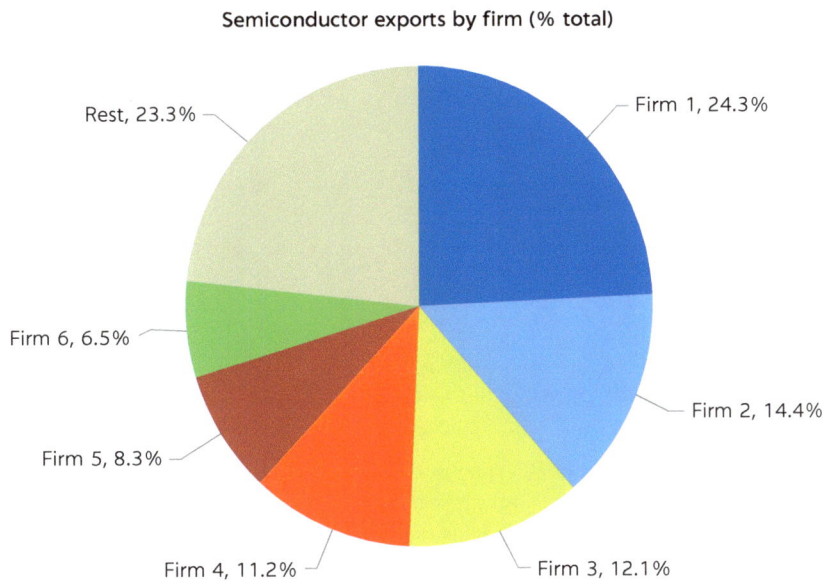

Rest, 23.3%
Firm 1, 24.3%
Firm 2, 14.4%
Firm 3, 12.1%
Firm 4, 11.2%
Firm 5, 8.3%
Firm 6, 6.5%

Source: Panjiva data.

RETHINKING THE PHILIPPINES' GVC PARTICIPATION IN THE IMT, TMT, AND HLS CLUSTERS

To increase its participation in the IMT, TMT, and HLS clusters, the Philippines needs to address many challenges. This discussion of the opportunities and challenges is based on four sources of information:

1. A sector analysis and profile conducted through the lens of COVID-19, GVCs, and megatrends.
2. A combination of cluster mapping and value chain analysis (included in the sector analysis).
3. An update of the 2019 sector scan conducted jointly by the Philippines Board of Investments and the World Bank, focusing initially on the IMT, TMT, and HLS clusters broken down into 16 subsectors, with a weighting for GVC and policy integrated into the scoring matrix.
4. Interviews conducted with 56 companies covering the three GVC clusters. Although the response rate was only 23 percent, the caliber of interviewees was very high. The interviews generated cogent intelligence that was distilled into the discussion without explicit attribution to preserve confidentiality.

Industrial, manufacturing, and transportation

The Philippines has a unique opportunity to increase its participation in the aerospace subsector. The recent developments at the global level in maintenance, repair, and operations and the electric vehicle industry (figure 2.10) and the semiconductor industry (figure 2.11) augur well for the Philippines.

FIGURE 2.10

FIGURE 2.10

Market share and revenue for the maintenance, repair, and operations and electric vehicle markets at the global level, 2018–26

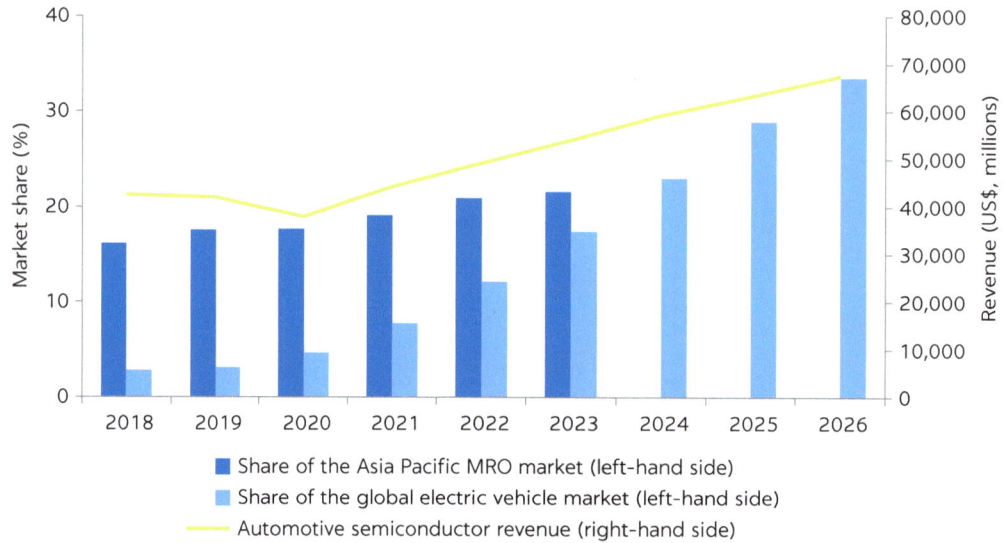

- Share of the Asia Pacific MRO market (left-hand side)
- Share of the global electric vehicle market (left-hand side)
- Automotive semiconductor revenue (right-hand side)

Source: Canalys, IHS Markit, and VLSI Research data.
Note: MRO = maintenance, repair, and operations.

FIGURE 2.11

Year-on-year growth of semiconductor equipment sales at the global level, by subsector, 2018–21

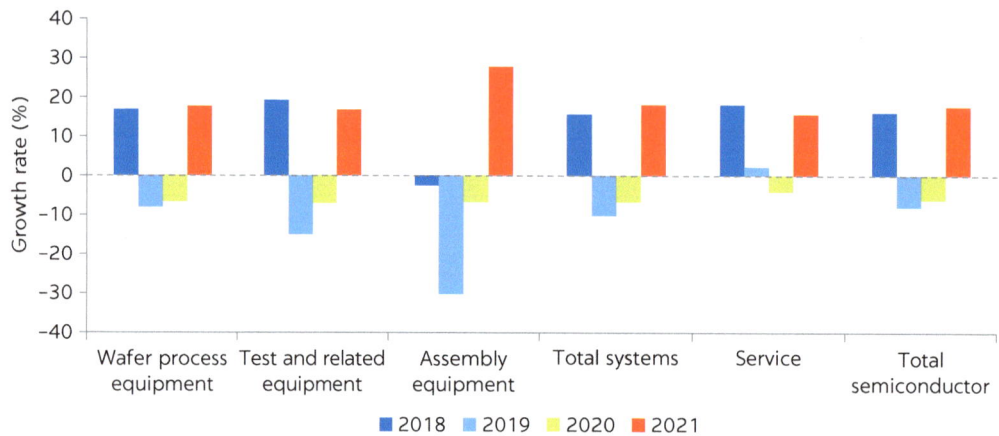

■ 2018 ■ 2019 ■ 2020 ■ 2021

Source: Canalys, IHS Markit, and VLSI Research data.

Indeed, the country hosts the leading global aircraft interior company, Collins Aerospace, and the world's leading maintenance, repair, and operations company, Lufthansa Technik. However, the country has been unable to attract other large companies to expand the cluster. Japan's involvement in production of the Boeing 787 aircraft and China's 2020 launch of its 737 competitor—the COMAC C919—will strengthen regional aerospace value chains and open opportunities for countries like the Philippines to participate and upgrade.

A shift away from fault tolerance in the aerospace industry also opens up opportunities for the Philippines. Fault tolerance has changed, as the resilience of critical electronic components and systems has improved, along with the fail-safe characteristics needed for safe autonomous driving. Thus, the three IMT sectors combined have increasing commonalities from, for example, the spike in demand for semiconductors, given the far higher technical specifications of integrated circuits than those found in smartphones and laptops, and for the bedrock skills needed to remain competitive. Based on investor feedback, universities have become more responsive to the needs of industry. Nevertheless, the aerospace sector still faces major challenges related to sourcing raw materials from abroad (frequent customs delays when sourcing advanced composites, which may not have been coded in the Philippines) and sourcing from local precision engineering companies.

To develop the aerospace industry, the Philippines needs to have a clear policy and strategy: a clear policy articulating what the sector should look like by 2030 and a strategy for promoting the country to the target audience. The gap between the needs of the few first-tier aerospace companies in the Philippines and the ability of local companies to satisfy precision machine tasks is too wide for a links intervention to bridge. Given the difficulties that local companies have in meeting the certification thresholds set by tier-one aviation companies in the Philippines, the Board of Investments should focus on attracting tier-two and tier-three investors, making it easier for local companies to participate in regional and global value chains.

Electronics investors interviewed in 2018 said that sector strategies and road maps were no substitute for a cogent, coherent, and time-bound policy (World Bank 2018). There is a policy vacuum, and the GVC reconfiguration initiative can serve as the departure point for an IMT Policy 2030. The semiconductor industry in the Philippines focuses on the segment with the tightest operational margins and greatest exposure to disruptive technologies: outsourced semiconductor assembly and test. Although 5G and the Internet of Things will benefit that segment, to sustain competitiveness and benefit fully from the Internet of Things, much more emphasis is needed on design and test, necessitating higher-level computer science skills. A group of foreign electronic manufacturing services (EMS) companies invested 20 years ago. While the Philippines hosts a couple of very successful domestic EMS multinational companies, greenfield EMS investors have largely steered clear of the Philippines over the last decade. Not only are employment opportunities being lost, but so too are opportunities to trigger productivity and innovation spillovers associated with the most recent wave of investment by the global top 25 EMS companies. Both the semiconductor and EMS sectors in the Philippines need to be on a higher trajectory to enhance innovation and boost value added. Policy action is urgently needed.

Countries like the Philippines that are struggling to be a profitable base for high-volume conventional vehicle production are unlikely to transition to high-volume production of electric vehicles. The Philippines needs a new business model, and automotive outsourcing could be the optimal model based on recent trends. Electric vehicles are the biggest driver of change worldwide, yet the Philippines is already a late entrant. Competing countries like Indonesia have already announced a target of building 600,000 electric vehicles by 2030. Toyota Motors Philippines has always been firmly committed to increasing local sourcing, but it has struggled to find local companies with the competency and capacity to meet its quality standards. As a result, 44 of the company's 473 suppliers in 2018 had a presence in the Philippines, but only half of those companies were locally owned. Few, if any, domestic automotive companies have outwardly invested, with Mitsubishi and Toyota helping local companies to integrate into their own supply chains, especially those supplying plants in Thailand.

Putting more emphasis on value addition and GVC integration moves the focus away from the domestic market. The Philippine government has sought to protect its domestic market, hiking import tariffs on new vehicles within two months of signing the Regional Comprehensive Economic Partnership agreement. The country has some assets to support a competitive electric vehicle industry, including voluminous quartz and cobalt resources, which can be converted into lithium-ion batteries, and strengths in electronics, which can be leveraged to support the transition into electronic systems and subassemblies for electric vehicles.[1] In addition, designing customized integrated circuits for automotive original equipment manufacturers and attracting an automotive outsourcing facility to form the core of a mega automotive cluster are also important. To achieve this goal, a clear automotive policy is needed.

These developments suggest that addressing the policy vacuum for an integrated IMT cluster is a priority. Several commonalities and interdependencies are weighing on the competitiveness of the aerospace, electronics, and automotive sectors. These factors include lack of skills, inadequate enabling environment, weak market accessibility and connectivity, high overhead, cost inefficiencies, property requirements, highly mobile foreign direct investment, and lack of clear policies in all three sectors. Consequently, the GVC reconfiguration initiative can represent the fulcrum for an IMT Policy 2030 for the Philippines by combining the three sectors on the premise that "a rising tide lifts all boats."

Technology, media, and telecommunications

Two decades ago, the Philippines presented call center and BPO investors with a very compelling value proposition, offering competitive costs, an educated workforce, cultural and linguistic affinity with customers in many time zones, incentives, and professional investor services of the Philippine Economic Zone Authority. Currently, the BPO and shared services segment employs about 1.3 million Filipinos, producing close to US$30 billion in revenue. The segment was running at 95 percent productivity during the COVID-19 crisis. However, the BPO sector is more customer service oriented (voice), while analytics and related tasks are relatively small in the Philippines compared to countries such as Poland (figure 2.12). Although automation is still a risk, service offshoring—notably knowledge process outsourcing such as health care and animation game development—is expected to grow rapidly (figure 2.13).

The BPO segment proved to be relatively resilient during the COVID-19 pandemic, achieving 95 percent of pre-pandemic levels of productivity by late 2020. Before the pandemic, the main challenge facing the sector was exceptionally high staff attrition. After receiving employer support to improve their analytical skills, many employees would move to other companies. Moreover, the switch to working from home had started before COVID-19, but companies were severely hampered by poor internet connectivity. Unlike competing locations that tended to be strong across the spectrum of information technology–enabled services (that is, BPO, information technology outsourcing, and knowledge process outsourcing), the Philippines is strong only in BPO. However, the Philippines still offers a compelling value proposition for shared services centers that support global operations and BPO activities that support and enhance the GVC

FIGURE 2.12

Business process outsourcing jobs in select countries, by type of job, 2017

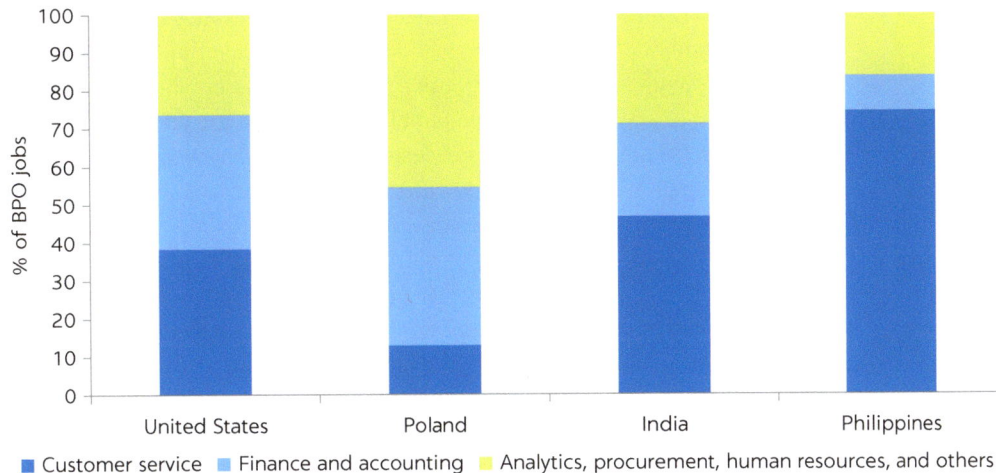

Source: A. T. Kearney Analysis 2017.
Note: BPO = business process outsourcing.

FIGURE 2.13

Projected growth of employment in the business process outsourcing sector in the Philippines, 2019–22

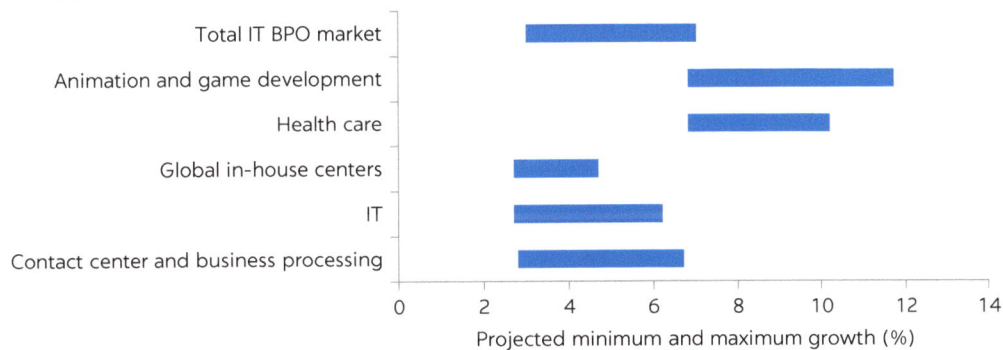

Source: IBPAP 2019.
Note: BPO = business process outsourcing; IT = information technology.

efficiencies of the verticals being supported. The Strategic Investments Priorities Plan, which is the list of sectors that qualify for incentives under the Corporate Recovery and Tax Incentives for Enterprise (CREATE) Act, should highlight the importance of investing in skills development for big data analytics and place more emphasis on investing in telecommunication infrastructure. One of the BPO companies interviewed for this study employs more than 90,000 people in the Philippines and is the country's largest private sector employer.

Some donors have advised the Board of Investments to target more BPO investment. This is not optimal. Given the very high staff attrition rates before COVID-19, the focus should be on motivating the impressive stock of international and domestic investors to upgrade to big data analytics while steering investments to shared services centers and knowledge process outsourcing. For BPO centers whose own value proposition is overly dependent on cost savings, voice, and low labor costs, it will become increasingly challenging for the Philippines to remain competitive. Nevertheless, call center jobs are still important, given high youth unemployment in the country.

These developments suggest that upgrading the BPO sector is a key step toward achieving an integrated TMT cluster. The focus should be on enabling existing BPO centers to upgrade into analytics. When it comes to BPO centers supporting other GVCs of relevance to the Philippines, scaled-up efforts to market the Philippines as globally competitive for shared services while accelerating the provision of skills and development of infrastructure are critical. In policy terms, the cross-cutting nature of the clusters means that an overarching digitalization policy should optimally guide further development of the TMT cluster.

Health and life sciences

The Philippines hosts about 60 of the top 100 pharmaceutical companies in the world, but only a couple of them manufacture in the Philippines. Furthermore, between 2015 and 2020, the Philippines did not attract any foreign investors in pharmaceutical manufacturing. With both foreign pharmaceutical companies and large domestic companies focusing so sharply on the domestic market—the third largest pharmaceutical market in the Association of Southeast Asian Nations—the Philippines' participation in the pharmaceutical GVC is the most tenuous of all the cluster GVCs. The trade imbalance is stark. For 2019, pharmaceutical imports amounted to more than US$1.8 billion, while corresponding exports were 33 times less, at US$55 million. In interviews, one of the major international pharmaceutical companies said that its molecules are too complex to manufacture locally and that exporting is difficult due to lack of cost efficiencies and poor connectivity. Based on investor feedback, the drug approvals authority is neither as efficient nor as business friendly as authorities in competing countries. The Philippine Food and Drug Administration licensing policies are quite bureaucratic and difficult to manage for pharmaceuticals and medical devices. The life sciences subsector has not developed, and, until it does, the country will miss out on future biopharmaceutical growth. As figures 2.14 and 2.15 suggest, tapping into the role of multinational corporations operating in the sector and harnessing the country's relative strength in the BPO sector could help to position the Philippines in the telehealth and telemedicine subsectors.

Three policy issues are pressing: (a) motivating the extensive cadre of cross-border investors to manufacture in the Philippines, (b) enabling domestic companies to export from the Philippines, and (c) nurturing the development of a life sciences and biotechnology industry. In the absence of such policies, the Philippines will miss out on the next generation of biopharmaceuticals investment. For the first issue, the immediate solution is for domestic companies to increase their "toll manufacturing" capacity, leveraging the scale effect from the country's large local market; the second and third issues are more complex and will require a policy for the HLS cluster.

These developments suggest that patient care and leveraging the BPO sector are key to increasing the Philippines' participation in the HLS cluster. For instance, telemedicine apps could be a mode for exporting basic diagnostics to other countries, leveraging the country's cost advantage and English language proficiency as well as the high insurance costs in export markets such as the United States. However, focusing first on the certification and regulatory environment and then on taking the biotech industry from the "petri dish" to special economic zones dedicated to life sciences could support the country's presence in the pharmaceutical subsector. The key to exporting is to aim for US Food and Drug Administration (FDA) approval. Based on FDA data, 136,400 foreign

FIGURE 2.14

Share of total value of sales in the health and life sciences sector in the Philippines, by type of corporation, 2007–16

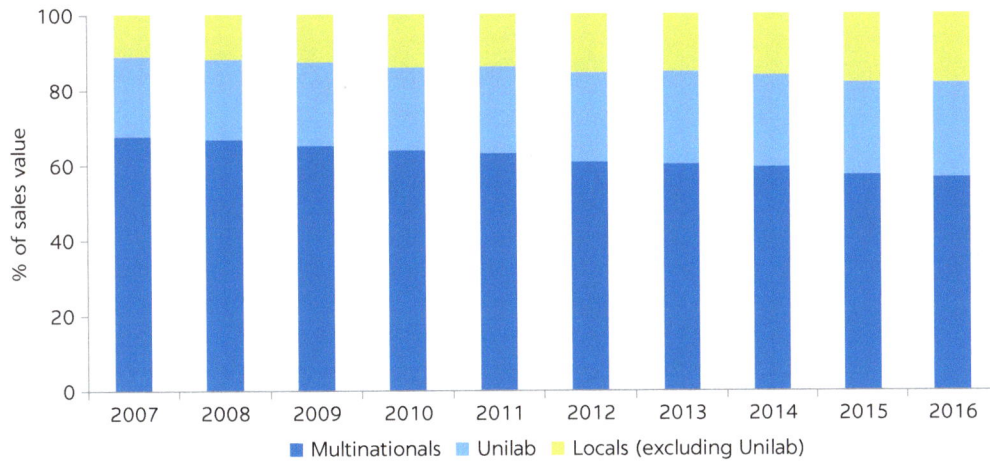

Source: Based on IQVIA Philippines data.

FIGURE 2.15

Projected value of the Asia Pacific Internet of Things health care market, 2020–27

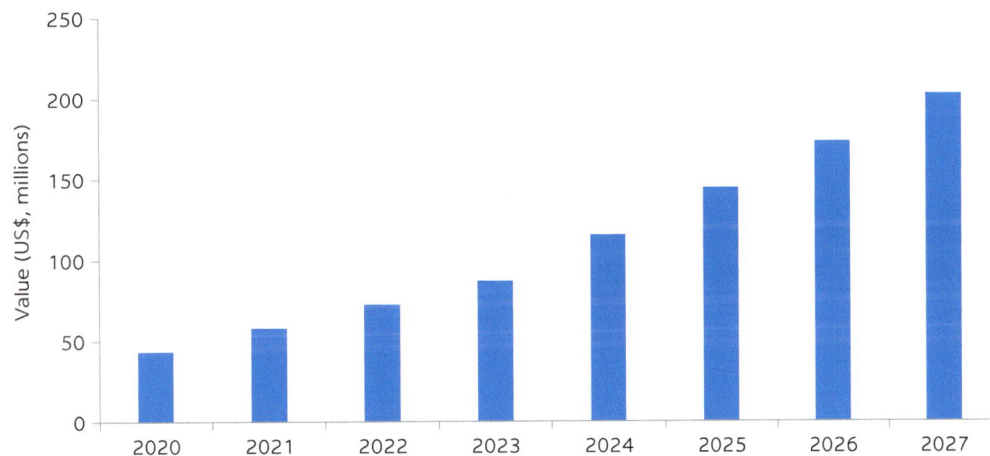

Source: Data Bridge Market Research.

facilities in more than 150 countries export FDA-regulated products to the United States, following foreign inspections and collaboration between the FDA and host-country counterparts. FDA approval represents a gateway into other markets in the region.

A thorough understanding of the attributes and conditions of successful biotechnology clusters outside of established areas of innovation, like California or Munich, would also be helpful. Preconditions for success include a core cluster, which is a local base of knowledge (routinely a prominent university and commercial spinoffs), an innovation ecosystem (research and development funding, venture capital, and specialist services), and infrastructure for clinical trials (animal testing, human testing, and certification). Given the complexity of the task and the fact that the Philippines is starting from a low base, a comprehensive policy should work back from where the sector should be by 2030.

NOTE

1. Indonesia is leveraging its nickel assets to attract battery manufacturers from the Philippines. The Philippines also has large deposits of nickel.

REFERENCES

A. T. Kearney Analysis. 2017. "The Widening Impact of Automation." A. T. Kearney Analysis, Chicago, IL. https://www.kearney.com/documents/20152/793366/The+Widening +Impact+of+Automation.pdf/42b06cf4-e5f9-d8ec-a30c-a82dd26d4953.

IBPAP (IT & Business Process Association of the Philippines). 2019. "The Philippine IT-BPM Industry Growth Forecast (2019–2022)." Presentation, IBPAP, Bonifacio Global City, November 2019. https://www.ibpap.org/knowledge-hub.

Qiang, Christine Zhenwei, Yan Liu, and Victor Steenbergen. 2021. *An Investment Perspective on Global Value Chains*. Washington, DC: World Bank.

World Bank. 2018. "Multinational Companies Survey 2018." Unpublished manuscript, World Bank, Washington, DC.

World Bank. 2020a. *Philippines Digital Economy Report 2020: A Better Normal under COVID-19; Digitalizing the Philippine Economy Now*. Washington, DC: World Bank.

World Bank. 2020b. *World Development Report 2020: Trading for Development in the Age of Global Value Chains*. Washington, DC: World Bank.

3 Constraints and Opportunities for Increased GVC Participation

Current structural constraints will determine the participation of the Philippines in global value chains (GVCs) after COVID-19 (coronavirus). The COVID-19 supply shock differed from previous shocks in its pattern of propagation. Unlike two shocks to GVCs in 2011,[1] the effect of the virus did not depend on a location's proximity to one epicenter. Instead, in its early phase, the virus was disseminated along the routes of aircraft and cruise ships.

Firms in GVCs are making decisions to improve their economic efficiency in an environment of more frequent negative external shocks and greater policy uncertainty. On the one hand, shorter value chains, in which production is integrated at one location, tend to be more resilient in that, once the shock has passed, activities can resume more quickly. On the other hand, depending exclusively on suppliers from any one nation can increase risk, as is the case of Japan (Baldwin and Weder di Maura 2020). Complex supply chains can be a source of higher risks, but they also can provide a network of trading partners and economic gains that facilitate recovery. The substitutability of inputs is also a critical determinant of supply chain shocks, as it is possible for alternatives to replace imported intermediates in the short run (Boehm, Flaaen, and Pandalai-Nayar 2019). The resilience of GVCs and how they might be reconfigured in the Philippines will depend on these factors.

TRADE-RELATED CONSTRAINTS AND OPPORTUNITIES

Trade costs in the Philippines are some of the highest in the Association of Southeast Asian Nations (ASEAN), making physical connectivity a major constraint for GVC participation. These weaknesses were exacerbated within days of implementation of the extended community quarantine, with the international port of Manila becoming congested as consignees were unable to collect their containers from the port. The lack of an integrated trade information system made it difficult to assess whether cargo delays were due primarily to private sector issues (such as the lack of trucks, closed warehouses and factories, missing documentation from shipping lines) or to delays in obtaining clearances from trade-related government agencies.

The COVID-19 crisis, however, provided a unique opportunity to accelerate reforms on these issues. Indeed, during the height of the quarantine in April 2020, the Department of Finance, Department of Agriculture, Department of Trade and Industry, Bureau of Customs, and Philippines Ports Authority issued an administrative order expediting the release of cargo and requiring consignees or importers to pull out containers left in ports. This issuance addressed both logistical and administrative constraints.[2] Although clearance times remain relatively substantial, the Bureau of Customs has taken steps to streamline and automate the import clearance requirements, helping to reduce clearance times at the Manila International Container Terminal from 10 days and 19 hours in 2019 to 6 days and 3 hours in 2020.

Congestion in Manila puts the Philippines at a disadvantage in time-sensitive GVCs such as industrial, manufacturing, and transportation (IMT); technology, media, and telecommunication (TMT); and health and life sciences (HLS). Congestion in Manila is the result of many factors, including the lack of an efficient urban mass transit system, but the ban on heavy trucks during certain hours significantly affects the time and cost of operations, not only by shortening the window of operations but also by increasing the number of idle trucks congesting streets. The truck ban also results in trucks and truck drivers needing parking areas and rest facilities. In the absence of these services, most drivers park at gasoline stations and on nearby streets, adding to the congestion. Interviews with key players suggest that delays in being assigned to a container yard increase the idle time for trucks laden with empty containers. This situation is due, in part, to the country's trade imbalance: the number of imports is significantly greater than the number of exports, leading to a surplus of empty containers.

The Bureau of Customs has fast-tracked the digitalization of customs processing and payment transactions. It began to upgrade its customs processing system in 2018, including requiring the mandatory automation of operations, establishing the Bureau of Customs Operations Center, and undertaking digital transformation initiatives such as a customer care portal. However, the COVID-19 outbreak placed greater importance on streamlining trade-related procedures, motivating policy makers to speed reforms. With imposition of the extended community quarantine, the Bureau of Customs fast-tracked the immediate adoption of emergency protocols, such as online filing, processing of incomplete applications, mandatory acceptance of digital payments, and creation of a one-stop clearinghouse for medical supplies. The automation and digitalization of the customs process was expanded to include other port-related transactions, such as payments for cargo handling, storage, and transportation scheduling, through the issuance of a joint memorandum in July 2020. The automation of processes by the Bureau of Customs and other port service providers will improve accountability, reduce face-to-face interactions, reduce delays, and minimize discretionary action by government officials.

The main constraints to the standardization of processes and products in the Philippines are technical barriers to trade. Technical regulations and standards and conformity assessments help to ensure the quality of exports; to protect health, the environment, and human, animal, and plant life; and to prevent deceptive practices. When they become abnormally restrictive, however, they become nontariff barriers subject to arbitration of the World Trade Organization. In the Philippines, about 43 such measures are imposed by at least 18 agencies supervised by 12 departments, a fragmentation that is constraining the country's ability to integrate smoothly into GVCs (World Bank 2020a). Export-related measures are imposed by 26 trade-related government agencies supervised by 10 departments and involve at least 85 such measures.

A review of the nontariff measures regulating Philippine exports and imports indicates that some of the measures adopted and implemented may restrict trade. The review finds a lack of clarity in the terminologies used, as most of the measures are classified loosely as accreditations, licenses to operate, registrations, certificates of authority, permits, or clearances. Some commodities are regulated by several trade-related government agencies, with overlapping or confusing legal rules. In several instances, some commodities are regulated collectively by multiple agencies; importers and exporters sometimes have to visit each agency in person and submit hard copies of the same documents.

To enhance transparency and streamline the permitting process for these nontariff measures, the Philippines established the Philippine National Trade Repository and TradeNet. In August 2017, the Department of Trade and Industry launched a repository that consolidates comprehensive, up-to-date information on trade-related matters, allowing companies to use a single portal to access the permits and regulations required to import and export their particular products across government agencies. That same year, the Department of Finance began the process of establishing TradeNet—the Philippine national single window—to create an online portal for automating the issuance of permits by trade-related government agencies. The Philippines had established a national single window in 2009, but the program was not fully integrated, with only 10 agencies using it as of 2016. In 2015, the Department of Finance developed the Inter-Agency Business Interoperability project team to simplify import and export procedures and the documentary requirements of trade-related government agencies. This project team remains committed to establishing TradeNet, with the help of the customs commissioner and the Anti-Red Tape Authority.

The COVID-19 crisis accelerated these trade facilitation reforms. For instance, in relation to the Philippines' commitment under the World Trade Organization's trade facilitation agreement, the Philippines established the Philippine Trade Facilitation Committee by virtue of Executive Order 136, s.2021 issued on May 18, 2021. The committee is tasked with streamlining trade processes and improving customs operations, which will lower the cost of trade transactions and enable micro, small, and medium enterprises to participate more in international trade. TradeNet is already operational, with four agencies able to receive and process documents. Meanwhile, as of December 2021, 18 additional agencies have completed the onboarding stage and are waiting to be deployed in the production environment for live implementation. The remaining agencies will be undertaking preparatory activities in 2022. The TradeNet platform is also connected to the ASEAN single window; as of November 2021, the Philippines had completed its preliminary activities and testing of connectivity and is now set to join other member states in exchanging the ASEAN customs declaration document electronically. Scaling up these efforts to address specific logistical constraints faced in the IMT, TMT, and HLS clusters will facilitate the Philippines' GVC participation in these strategic sectors.

The Philippines has signed some free trade agreements, including the Regional Comprehensive Economic Partnership (RCEP) agreement.[3] Signed on November 15, 2020, the RCEP is the world's largest free trade agreement, encompassing 30 percent of global gross domestic product (GDP), 27 percent of global merchandise trade, more than 18 percent of services trade, and 19 percent of foreign direct investment (FDI) outflows. The agreement deepens trade and investment between member countries mainly through reductions in nontrade barriers on goods and services. It harmonizes the provisions imposed by countries on trade in goods, providing more certainty for traders and investors. For example, it encourages importing countries to accept the product standards of exporting countries if those countries are RCEP members and provide the same level of consumer protection.

The RCEP aligns rules of origin for all 15 countries, allowing participants to integrate into the same production chain. This may help the RCEP to attract a larger share of GVCs and each country to deepen specialization, an important development at a time when the reconfiguration of GVCs in and out of China has been accelerated by the China-US trade dispute and increasing geopolitical threats to the semiconductor industry. The RCEP contains relatively strong provisions to protect intellectual property, which may help to allay the concerns of international investors, in particular, in Southeast Asian countries. However, a significant carve-out in the area of electronic commerce for national security concerns may limit the degree to which these provisions are binding on China and some other members. The RCEP covers relevant provisions in services too, including commitments by each member not to discriminate against other members' investors in several service sectors. Finally, it facilitates the temporary movement of persons for investment and trade activities.

Although its benefits might not be immediate for some sectors or firms, rapid implementation of the RCEP would be a move in the right direction. The Department of Trade and Industry projects that the main benefit from the RCEP will come from better trade facilitation (one agreement and uniform rules to follow across countries) and estimates US$60 billion in additional exports by 2025. However, the automotive sector in the Philippines views the RCEP as a potential threat because it makes complementarity across ASEAN countries less and less meaningful in the sector. Moreover, the country already has free trade agreements with various countries as well as an agreement with the United States (under the Generalized System of Preferences), so the RCEP may not bring many new advantages. The electronics sector echoes this opinion and does not see any drastic changes. For the personal protective equipment sector, the RCEP offers opportunities in large markets. But the challenge is to become more competitive, especially because countries within the RCEP will also compete on low labor costs, like Cambodia and the Lao People's Democratic Republic. Yet the RCEP does bring some business opportunities because it includes some large high-income markets in which health services business processing outsourcing (BPO) is required. Some members of the Healthcare Information Management Association of the Philippines have clients in Australia, but work is limited in other RCEP countries. The main challenge is to develop skills to support a competitive digital health care offering (telehealth and telemedicine services) in these destinations.

FDI-RELATED CONSTRAINTS AND OPPORTUNITIES

The Organisation for Economic Co-operation and Development's FDI Regulatory Restrictiveness Index gauges the restrictiveness of a country's FDI rules by looking at the four main types of restrictions: foreign equity limitations, screening or approval mechanisms, restrictions on the employment of foreigners as key personnel, and operational restrictions, such as restrictions on branching, capital repatriation, or landownership (OECD 2018). In 2019, the Philippines was ranked as Asia's most restrictive country. Among the countries showcased in figure 3.1, the Philippines ranks the highest on the FDI Regulatory Restrictiveness Index for transportation and telecommunications. This ranking reflects the country's constitutional restriction on foreign ownership in these key sectors. The Philippines is also losing out to competing locations on many greenfield investments in manufacturing and services, which is a concern. A graver consequence, however, is the risk that more and more current foreign investors are reaching the inflection point beyond which management based in the Philippines will find it increasingly challenging to persuade headquarters (which see higher growth rates and profitability elsewhere) that they should remain committed to the Philippines. Furthermore, many FDI plants in the country are nearing the end of their economic life, which brings that inflection point even closer.

The Philippines is losing out to other ASEAN countries in attracting FDI, despite its competitive advantages. FDI inflows as a share of GDP climbed from 0.65 percent in 2010 to 2.78 percent in 2017, which was still only about half the ASEAN average (figure 3.2, panel a). While the Philippines is catching up with Malaysia and Thailand in FDI inflows, its FDI stock per capita is still much lower. In 2019, FDI stock per capita in the Philippines stood at US$810, which is 50 percent lower than in Vietnam, 80 percent lower than in Thailand, and 85 percent lower than in Malaysia (figure 3.2, panel b). Limitations on foreign ownership in many sectors constrain FDI in the Philippines; poor infrastructure, regulatory inconsistencies, and high energy costs are further disincentives to invest. However, the Philippines has many competitive advantages, such as an

FIGURE 3.1

FDI Regulatory Restrictiveness Index in select Asian countries, by sector, 2019

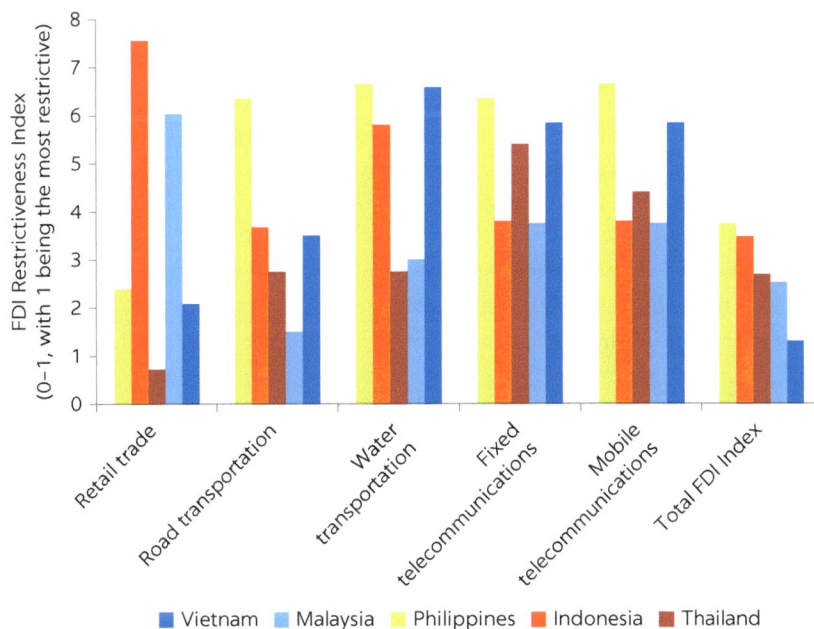

Source: Organisation for Economic Co-operation and Development (OECD) data.
Note: FDI = foreign direct investment.

FIGURE 3.2

Aggregate trends in foreign direct investment in the Philippines and select Asian countries

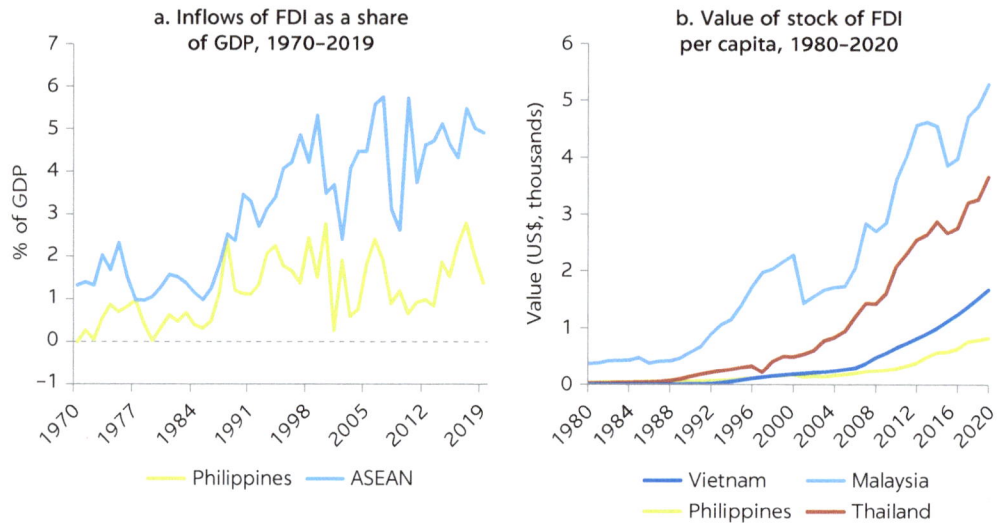

a. Inflows of FDI as a share of GDP, 1970–2019

b. Value of stock of FDI per capita, 1980–2020

Philippines — ASEAN

Vietnam — Malaysia
Philippines — Thailand

Source: United Nations Conference on Trade and Development (UNCTAD) data.
Note: ASEAN = Association of Southeast Asian Nations; FDI = foreign direct investment.

English-speaking workforce, strong cultural proximity to the United States, and a geographic advantage in the East Asia and Pacific region.

The Philippines' FDI performance in its key sectors was uneven during the past decade. FDI has been key to development of the electronics sector, the country's largest manufacturing export industry, although FDI inflows and exports were higher in ASEAN peers such as Malaysia, Thailand, and Vietnam. The BPO sector is one of the most dynamic and fastest-growing industries in the Philippines, providing good jobs to millions of workers and driving economic growth. FDI inflows to this sector have been consistently higher in the Philippines than in its peers. Unlike electronics, the automotive industry is domestically oriented, except for wiring harnesses. Policies to attract lead firms and FDI in the automotive sector to exports is a strategic move that stakeholders in the sector could consider.

The impact of COVID-19 on global FDI has been significant and may persist longer than the impact on trade. Global FDI, which was already in decline before the pandemic, fell by 42 percent in 2020, which is more than 30 percent below the drop that followed the 2008–09 global financial crisis (UNCTAD 2021). The pandemic's immediate impact on FDI stemmed from a reduction in reinvested earnings, as the affiliates of multinational companies experienced large drops in profits. Equity capital flows also shrank, as companies put new investment projects on hold amid travel bans, contractions in demand, a liquidity crunch, and greater uncertainty. The value of cross-border merger and acquisition deals was less affected, but announcements of greenfield FDI projects were down 89 percent in 2020. Although profits and reinvestment of earnings will increase as the pandemic subsides, investor confidence (and, by extension, new greenfield and merger and acquisition projects) may take longer to recover. This slow recovery may have long-term consequences for host economies, given FDI's role in development finance, knowledge transfer, and economic transformation (Qiang, Liu, and Steenbergen 2021).

Although total approved FDI in the Philippines declined between 2019 and 2020, there were positive developments. FDI declined from ₱390 billion in 2019 to ₱112 billion in 2020, down 71 percent, due to concerns and uncertainty surrounding the effect of a prolonged pandemic on the global economy as well as to travel restrictions for foreign nationals in the Philippines. Information and communication; electricity, gas, and steam; and manufacturing experienced the greatest declines in FDI, falling by ₱218,888 million, ₱70,281 million, and ₱24,181 million, respectively, from 2019 to 2020 (figure 3.3). However, FDI inflows from Taiwan, China; the United Kingdom; and the United States fueled modern services (including professional and scientific activities) and transportation, which are important segments of the HLS and IMT clusters. In light

FIGURE 3.3

Change in approved foreign direct investment in the Philippines, by sector, 2019–20

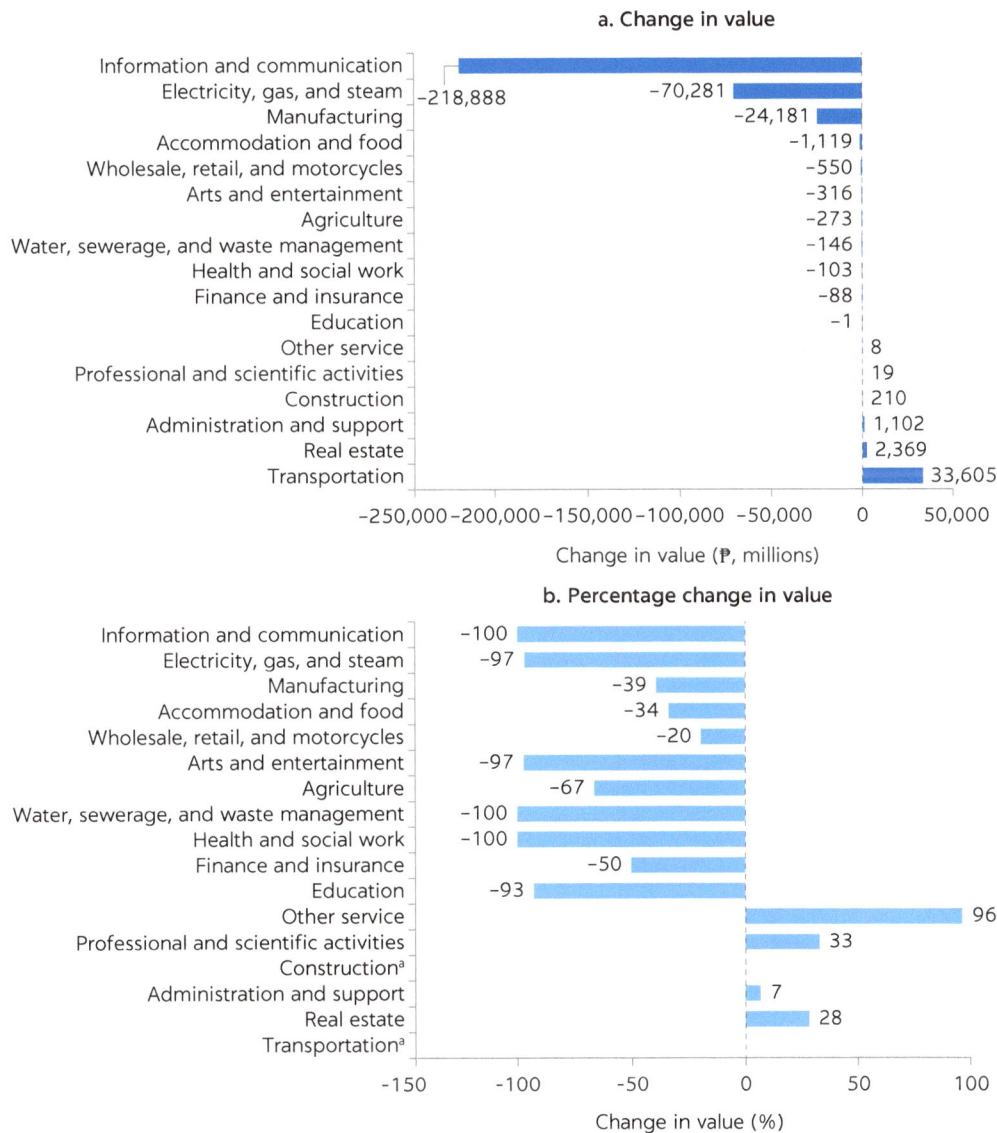

a. Change in value

Sector	Change in value (₱, millions)
Information and communication	−218,888
Electricity, gas, and steam	−70,281
Manufacturing	−24,181
Accommodation and food	−1,119
Wholesale, retail, and motorcycles	−550
Arts and entertainment	−316
Agriculture	−273
Water, sewerage, and waste management	−146
Health and social work	−103
Finance and insurance	−88
Education	−1
Other service	8
Professional and scientific activities	19
Construction	210
Administration and support	1,102
Real estate	2,369
Transportation	33,605

Change in value (₱, millions)

b. Percentage change in value

Sector	Change in value (%)
Information and communication	−100
Electricity, gas, and steam	−97
Manufacturing	−39
Accommodation and food	−34
Wholesale, retail, and motorcycles	−20
Arts and entertainment	−97
Agriculture	−67
Water, sewerage, and waste management	−100
Health and social work	−100
Finance and insurance	−50
Education	−93
Other service	96
Professional and scientific activities	33
Construction[a]	
Administration and support	7
Real estate	28
Transportation[a]	

Change in value (%)

Source: Calculations based on data from the Authority of the Freeport Area of Bataan, Board of Investments, Board of Investments–Bangsamoro Autonomous Region in Muslim Mindanao, Clark Development Corporation, Subic Bay Metropolitan Authority, Cagayan Economic Zone Authority, and Philippine Economic Zone Authority.
a. Outlier values omitted from figure.

of the COVID-19 crisis, an opportunity exists to revisit the policy framework governing these segments of the two clusters in order to identify entry points and encourage participation from foreign as well as domestic firms.

Three sectors had positive growth of FDI announcements in 2020 compared to the average for 2015–19: building materials, nonautomotive original equipment manufacturing, and paper, printing, and packaging (figure 3.4), possibly reflecting greater foreign investor confidence in these three sectors during

FIGURE 3.4

Greenfield foreign direct investment announcements, by sector

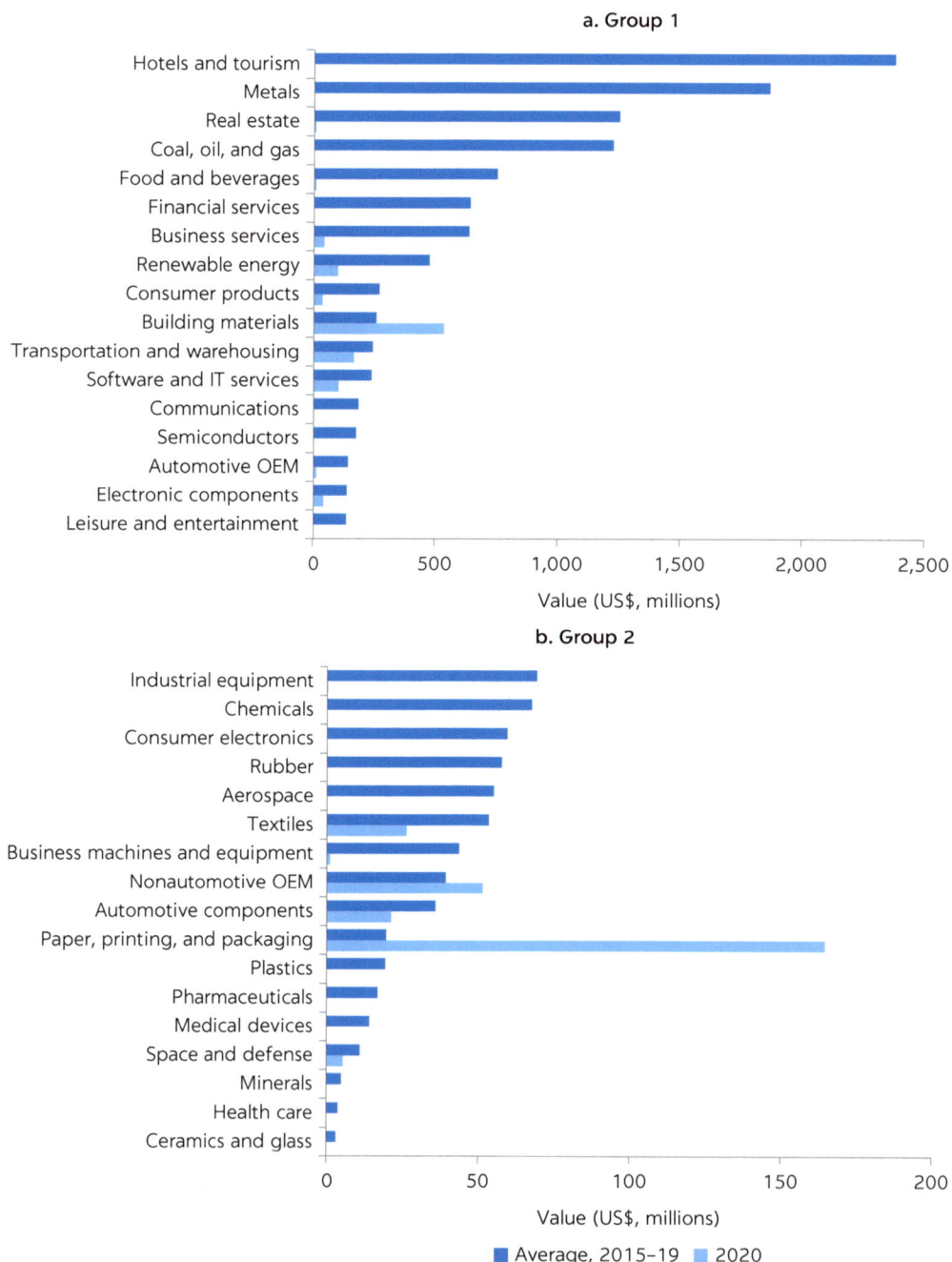

Source: World Bank calculations using FDI markets data.
Note: IT = information technology. OEM = original equipment manufacturing.

the pandemic. Of the three sectors, the nonautomotive original equipment manufacturing sector provides the most opportunity for the transportation equipment sector, reinforcing the strategic role of the IMT cluster for the country's prospects of GVC participation. In line with global trends, the COVID-19 pandemic caused FDI in the Philippines to plunge, but it also provided an opportunity to rethink the country's GVC participation strategy.

SKILLS-RELATED CONSTRAINTS AND OPPORTUNITIES

The nature of work has been changing rapidly as a result of advances in technology and globalization. Firms strive to adopt new technologies, markets expand, and societies evolve (figure 3.5; World Bank 2018). Businesses need to be innovative and flexible to survive in today's globalized economy, which is defined by cut-throat competition. Human capital is a critical element of technology adoption and the ability to maneuver in the ever-evolving global economy. Today's global structure of production is a fragmented process undertaken by a complex network of firms and countries specializing in different stages of production. COVID-19 could be a catalyst to speed up labor market changes in line with evolving global trends. In these areas, the Philippines is at a disadvantage vis-à-vis its regional peers (figure 3.6).

COVID-19 negatively affected capital and labor, but it also created an opportunity to retool and reskill workers. A significant decline in labor force participation in the first half of 2020 was almost offset by January 2021, with a noticeable increase in the number of information and communication technology (ICT) workers across sectors. Although the services sector is the largest employer, most of its workers have few skills, and the share of workers with postsecondary education has not increased over the last decade. Improving workers' skills in the service sector is crucial to improving GVC participation. By linking economies through firm-level collaboration, FDI is a source of both

FIGURE 3.5

Investment per capita in artificial intelligence companies in select countries, 2019

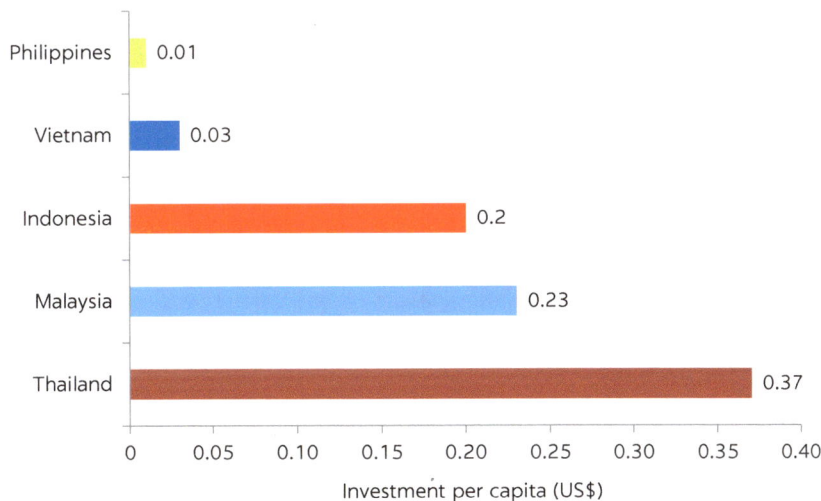

Source: A. T. Kearney 2019.

FIGURE 3.6

Difference between country score and regional average score for workforce skills in select countries, 2019

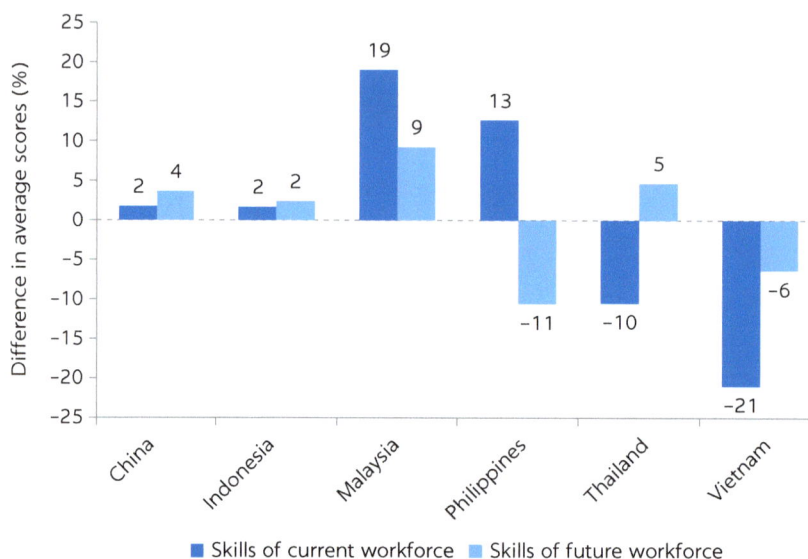

Source: WEF 2019b.

vulnerability and resilience. To improve economic recovery and create more jobs, it is important to enhance FDI's attractiveness by reviewing and promoting the country's FDI policy and by improving the business environment in general. Unfortunately, the Philippines attracts lower FDI inflows than peer countries partly due to restrictive policies.

In the Philippines, the share of nonroutine occupations has increased, while the share of routine occupations has declined. According to the International Labour Organization's 2020 estimate, which is based on the approach of Jaimovich and Siu (2020), the Philippines' share of nonroutine cognitive occupations rose from an estimated 21 percent to 24 percent, while the share of routine occupations fell from 34 percent to 31 percent between 2010 and 2016. The share of nonroutine manual occupations remained constant. The shift could be attributed to both automation and GVC participation. Moreover, the shift toward nonroutine occupations was driven by male workers, which calls for gendered retooling and reskilling policies.

Although the share of skilled workers in the service sector is growing, it is still lower than in the country's regional peers. Although the percentage of service sector exports is increasing, the increase is driven mainly by the BPO sector, which is currently at the lower end of the TMT cluster. To upgrade the position of the service sector, it is important to develop the right skills. Services exports have shifted toward more skill-intensive sectors over the last two decades, showing the potential to switch toward more advanced activities in the future. The lessons learned in the move up to the sectors requiring higher skills could be relevant when adopting more advanced, research and development–oriented, and complicated production systems in coming years.

The differentiated effect of COVID-19 across occupation groups suggests opportunities for the Philippines to expand its participation in the TMT cluster. Occupations that require more personal contact and frequent engagement suffered disproportionately during the pandemic. According to LinkedIn, the world's largest professional networking website, the top 10 emerging jobs in the Philippines are related to ICT and engineering. The top three emerging jobs are robotics engineer, cybersecurity specialist, and customer service specialist (LinkedIn 2020). COVID-19 also severely affected the arts, entertainment, and tourism industries (figure 3.7). At the same time, anecdotal evidence in the animation segment indicates emerging opportunities for the Philippines to

FIGURE 3.7

Changes in the composition of employment in the Philippines, by industry, January–July 2020

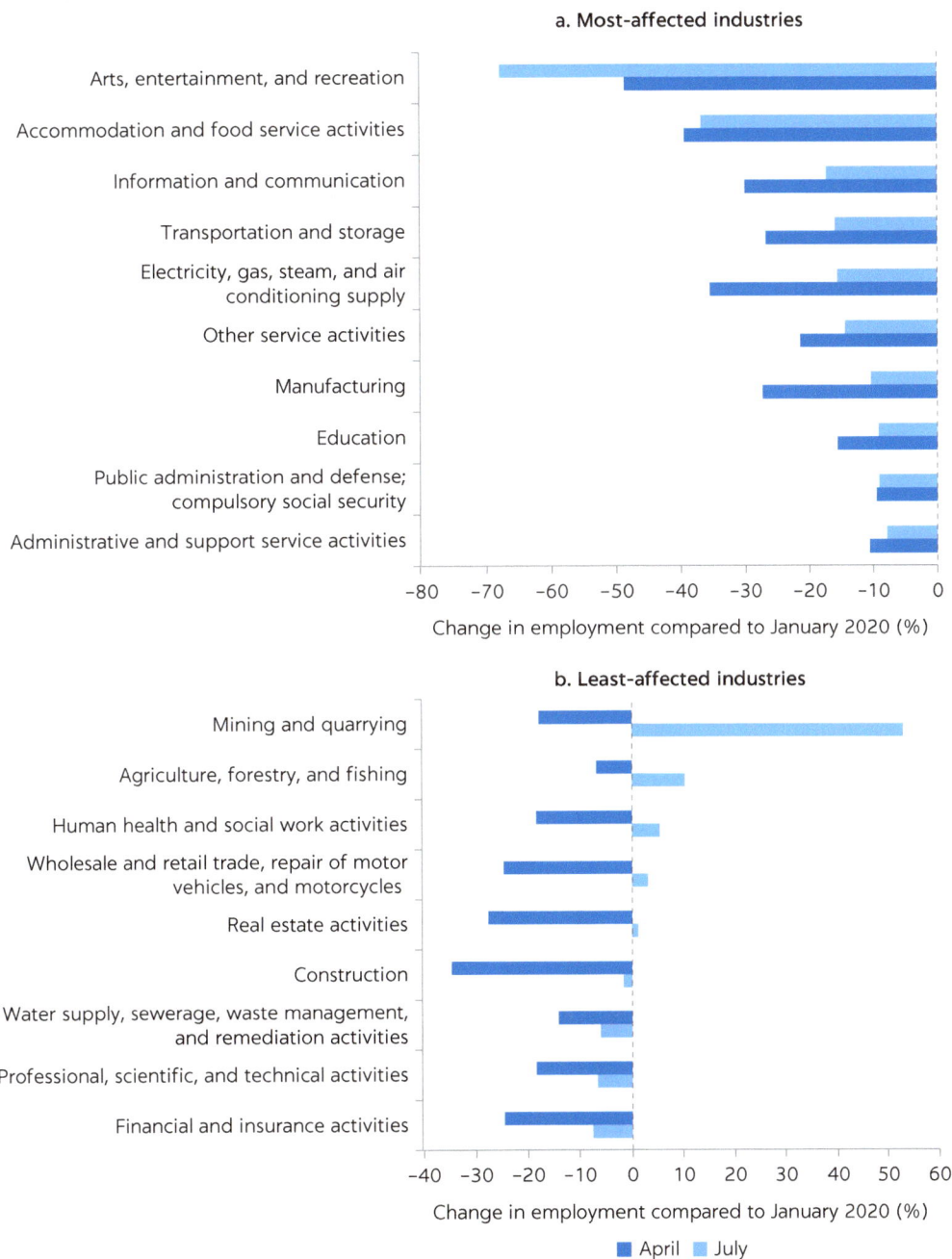

Source: World Bank staff based on the Philippines Labor Force Survey.

participate in the TMT cluster.[4] Creative services that involve original content, such as animation, software development, and game development, are also included in the Strategic Investments Priorities Plan of the Philippine Board of Investments, which entitles investors to incentives if they locate in the Philippines.

The pandemic led to a substantial increase in the share of trained ICT experts in many industries. Several factors contributed to this trend. First, the lockdown led to an unprecedented level of people working from home, which requires ICT experts to facilitate communication and help workers to complete complex tasks digitally and remotely. Second, firms may adopt technologies to cope with the pandemic's adverse effects by using automation and robotics to replace labor. As expected, more health experts were hired, and the share of nonuniversity graduates also rose substantially in many sectors (table 3.1). Demand for telehealth and telemedicine services increased during the COVID-19 pandemic, suggesting that the HLS cluster might be strategic. This cluster integrates pharmaceuticals, medical equipment, and health care services; and the Philippines is one of the top global providers of medical personnel.

The Philippines could provide regular training and mainstream lifelong learning as essential tools of upskilling and reskilling. More than 12 percent of young people in the Philippines believe that their knowledge is outdated, and 43 percent believe that their current knowledge needs to be updated (WEF 2019a). Compared to similar countries in the region, a relatively high percentage of young people think that their knowledge is obsolete. They recognize the importance of having up-to-date knowledge to functioning effectively in a modern, competitive, globalized economy. A survey of ASEAN youth, including Filipinos, shows that they lack proficiency in essential skills, such as software and programming skills as well as language skills. Technology changes quickly, and keeping abreast of new advances and being successful at a higher level of GVCs require constant updating of knowledge and skills. Establishing platforms to facilitate lifelong learning is critical. Despite the notable increase in the number of science, technology, engineering, and mathematics graduates, the education system needs to do a better job of matching its teaching to the evolving demands of labor markets to capture more lucrative parts of the value chain. It is also important to address youth unemployment and underemployment as well as the gender gap that may result from GVC reconfiguration and automation. Studies show that women are at a higher risk of working in jobs vulnerable to automation.

Focusing on improving workers' skills in the services sector is crucial to improving GVC participation in the Philippines. Using Organisation for Economic Co-operation and Development Trade in Value Added (TiVA) data and information from the Programme for the International Assessment of Adult Competencies survey, Grundke et al. (2017) show that, to improve participation in GVCs, workers' skill level in the services sector deserves greater attention. The services sector can export a larger share of its value added through indirect links than through direct ones. A positive relationship between skill intensity and backward GVC participation in complex production is evident in select service industries in the Philippines and comparator countries (figure 3.8). Moreover, despite the Philippines' relatively well-educated labor force in the business services sector, its backward GVC participation is lower than that of Malaysia, Thailand, and Vietnam. Barriers other than lack of appropriate skills could be preventing firms from participating in GVCs. In the ICT and financial

TABLE 3.1 Shifts in specialization (fields of study) across industries in the Philippines during COVID-19

INDUSTRY	AGRICULTURE, FORESTRY, FISHERIES, AND VETERINARY	BUSINESS, ADMINISTRATION, AND LAW	EDUCATION	ENGINEERING, MANUFACTURING, AND CONSTRUCTION	HEALTH AND WELFARE	ICT	NATURAL SCIENCES, MATHEMATICS, AND STATISTICS	OTHERS	SOCIAL SCIENCES AND HUMANITIES
Accommodation and food service activities	0.31	0.13	-0.13	-1.14	0.42	0.07	0.07	-0.43	0.70
Administrative and support service activities	-0.03	-0.60	-0.06	-1.28	-0.86	-1.45	0.86	3.43	-0.01
Agriculture, forestry, and fishing	0.11	-0.25	0.06	-0.43	0.02	0.16	-0.03	0.55	-0.19
Arts, entertainment, and recreation	-1.31	3.66	-1.02	-0.98	1.25	6.42	0.00	-7.01	-1.03
Construction	0.12	-0.39	0.12	-1.03	0.01	0.08	-0.06	1.13	0.02
Education	0.47	-0.49	-4.29	0.94	0.74	1.04	1.44	-0.45	0.59
Electricity, gas, steam, and air conditioning	2.60	1.51	-1.43	1.18	0.48	3.26	0.54	-5.60	-2.55
Financial and insurance activities	1.11	1.33	-1.87	-0.99	1.47	0.77	-0.51	-0.26	-1.04
Human health and social work activities	0.03	-1.02	-14.74	0.08	8.16	-0.17	-0.48	7.55	0.58
Information and communication	0.02	0.14	-1.09	-1.62	3.16	5.77	-0.55	-1.74	-4.08
Manufacturing	-0.09	-0.41	-0.19	-2.44	0.10	0.69	-0.19	3.22	-0.69
Mining and quarrying	0.47	-3.09	-0.27	-3.66	0.67	1.12	-0.72	4.75	0.72
Other service activities	0.09	-0.35	0.36	-0.74	0.03	0.17	-0.02	0.44	0.03
Professional, scientific, and technical activities	1.58	5.71	2.65	3.73	0.30	-4.12	1.29	-8.07	-3.07
Public administration and defense	0.91	-0.81	-6.01	-1.03	0.59	2.14	0.12	7.02	-2.93
Real estate activities	0.39	-10.08	-0.53	-4.25	-0.56	4.63	-0.03	9.09	1.35
Transportation and storage	0.14	-0.21	0.02	-2.52	-0.08	-0.18	0.11	3.08	-0.37
Water supply and waste management	0.60	7.30	3.60	-5.24	-3.29	2.83	0.00	0.26	-6.06
Wholesale and retail trade	-0.17	-0.93	0.04	-1.42	0.30	0.27	-0.23	2.69	-0.54

Source: World Bank staff calculations based on the Philippines Labor Force Survey data.
Note: Green and orange colors refer to an increase or decrease in share of workers with a particular educational background within an industry, respectively. The darker the color, the higher the magnitude of the change. Blue refers to a light increase or decrease in the number of workers with a particular background within an industry. ICT = information and communication technology.

FIGURE 3.8

Backward participation in complex global value chains in select countries, by skill level of workers, 2017

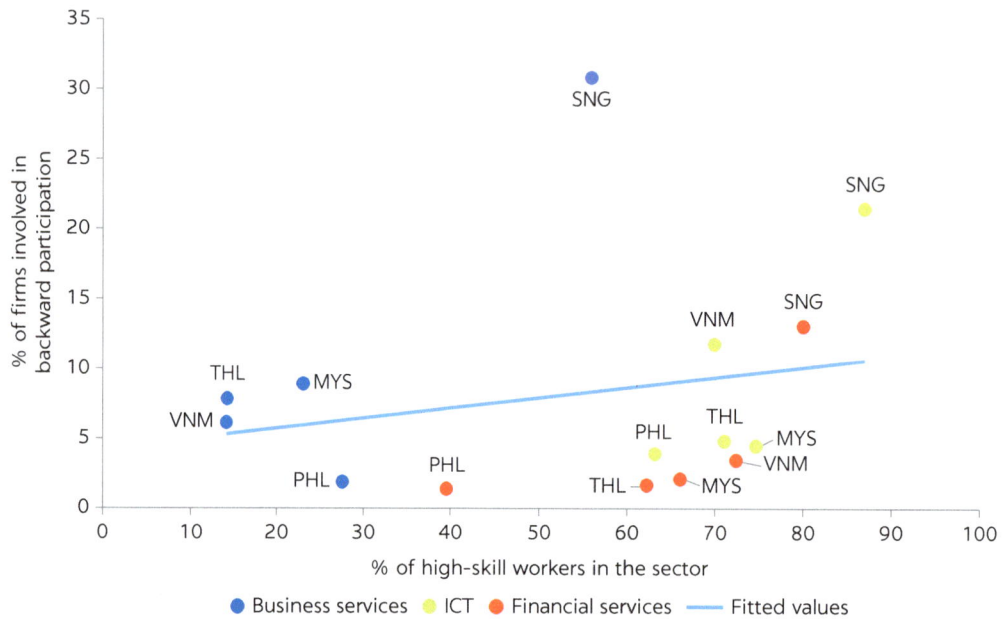

Source: Based on data from the Asian Development Bank (ADB) Key Indicators database and the International Labour Organization (ILO) ILOSTAT database.
Note: Covers employment in the business services, information and communication technology, and financial services sectors. ICT = information and communication technology.

services industries, the Philippines has a relatively lower-skill workforce and lower backward participation in GVCs. Hence, focus should be given to improving workers' skills in these industries. Other barriers should also be addressed, especially in business services.

Manufacturing of semiconductors and advanced electronics requires more highly skilled workers. Because the semiconductor industry is highly technical, it requires graduates with strong backgrounds in science, technology, engineering, and mathematics. The semiconductor industry is critical for a range of high-tech products, including smartphones, cars, and industrial equipment. Demand for these products will grow as artificial intelligence, quantum computing, and advanced communication technologies such as 5G evolve. So far, semiconductor fabrication is concentrated in the United States; Japan; the Republic of Korea; Singapore; Taiwan, China; and, recently, China. This very high market concentration is due to the skills required to excel in semiconductor production. For example, according to the Semi-Deloitte workforce survey (Deloitte 2018), engineering professionals in fields critical to the semiconductor industry are among the most difficult to hire. These fields include electrical engineering, computer sciences, software, mechanical, computer systems, materials sciences, and chemical engineering. These findings overlap significantly with LinkedIn's recent report on emerging jobs in the Philippine economy (LinkedIn 2020).

On average, the electrical equipment sector is skill intensive, but the skill intensity varies by subsector. For example, workers with lower skills can manufacture household appliances and electrical lighting, whereas workers with higher skills can make semiconductors, computers, and other high-tech goods (figure 3.9). The data suggest that, to move up the GVC and successfully produce such goods, a synchronized policy is needed to address the challenges in

FIGURE 3.9

Share of high-skill workers in select US manufacturing industries, 2019

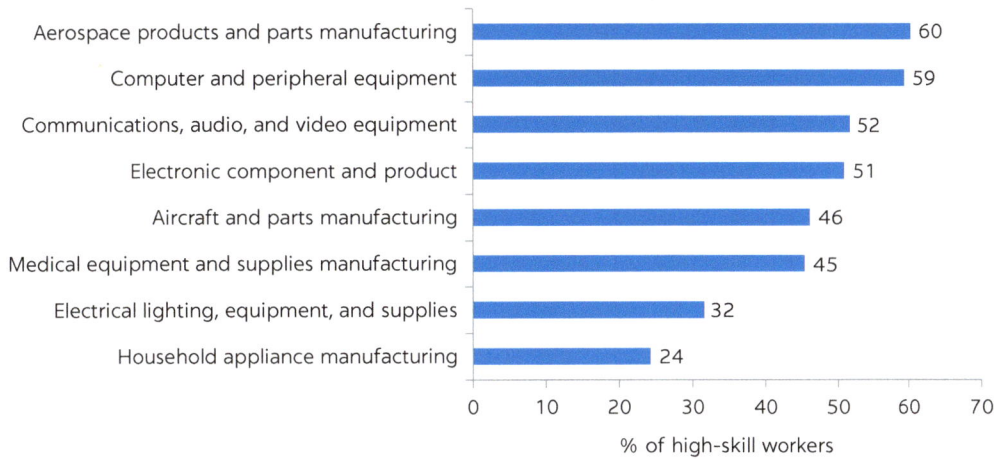

Source: World Bank staff based on Current Population Survey 2019 data.
Note: High skill refers to workers with at least a bachelor's degree.

the Philippine labor market, especially in science, technology, engineering, and mathematics. A short-term policy option could be to allow highly skilled immigrants to work in these areas. Moreover, maintaining highly qualified engineers and attracting overseas Filipino workers could play a positive role. According to Hunt and Zwetsloot (2020), about 2 percent of highly skilled workers in the US electronic components and products sector between 2012 and 2016 were from the Philippines.

Innovative firms in the Philippines have difficulty hiring workers with adequate skills. Nearly 80 percent of innovating firms in the Philippines cite a lack of managerial and leadership skills as a challenge when hiring new workers, while more than half cite work ethics and commitment, lack of interpersonal and communication skills, and scarcity of technical (non–information technology) skills. Between 20 and 40 percent of such firms cite computer, ICT, or foreign language skills as critical challenges when it comes to hiring (Cirera et al. 2021). This finding echoes a 2009 assessment of the training policies that the Commission on Higher Education, the Technical Education and Skills Development Authority, and the industry have to address employment mismatch (U-ACT 2009). The assessment identifies the following factors: lack of specialized qualifications and competencies, inadequate ICT skills, weak communication skills, poor work ethics and values, and inadequate experience, especially in highly specialized jobs. These structural constraints need to be addressed directly if the Philippines is to take advantage of ongoing reconfigurations in the IMT, TMT, and HLS clusters, given the increasing role of new technologies in these GVCs.

OTHER CONSTRAINTS AND OPPORTUNITIES

Although the financial market of the Philippines is quite liquid, access to credit by small and medium enterprises deteriorated during the COVID-19 pandemic. The total assets of the Philippine financial sector amount to 126 percent of GDP, of which the banking system holds about 94 percent (Cirera et al. 2021). Nonfinancial corporations are highly interconnected with the financial system through mixed structures that include nonfinancial corporations and banks. As of the end of 2018, about 80 percent of bank loans went to nonfinancial corporations, a much higher share than in other emerging economies (figure 3.10). Yet bank credit is just over 50 percent of GDP, as banks hold substantial liquid assets, which explains why the Philippines is ranked 132 out of 190 countries in the 2020 Doing Business report on getting credit, far behind regional averages. Despite the strong presence of conglomerates in the financing field, when it comes to maximizing value added and enhancing competitiveness, many conglomerates are averse to converting natural resources into primary and secondary export-oriented products. For instance, they tend to prefer retail, distribution, real estate development, and the mining and shipping of quartz rather than the conversion of copper oxide to meet the burgeoning demand for copper wire for electric vehicle motors.

Small and medium enterprises require access to a range of financial products suitable to their stage of development. They need to have access to three types of financial products: cash flow–based financing, asset-based financing, and viability-based financing (OECD 2015). Cash flow–based finance depends on the ability of lenders to assess the creditworthiness of firms and ascertain future earnings—hence the importance of having a credit reporting system through which lenders can access the credit histories of prospective borrowers. Asset-based debt financing instruments depend on the environment for secured transactions, namely, a comprehensive secured transaction framework, reliable and deep asset registries, and strong creditor rights. Viability-based financing allows small and medium enterprises with high growth potential to finance their growth with risk capital. Grouping asset-based and equity financing together as alternative sources of enterprise finance, the 2018 ASEAN Small and Medium Enterprise Policy Index yields a measure of the diversification of financing for

FIGURE 3.10

Credit to nonfinancial corporations in select countries, 2018

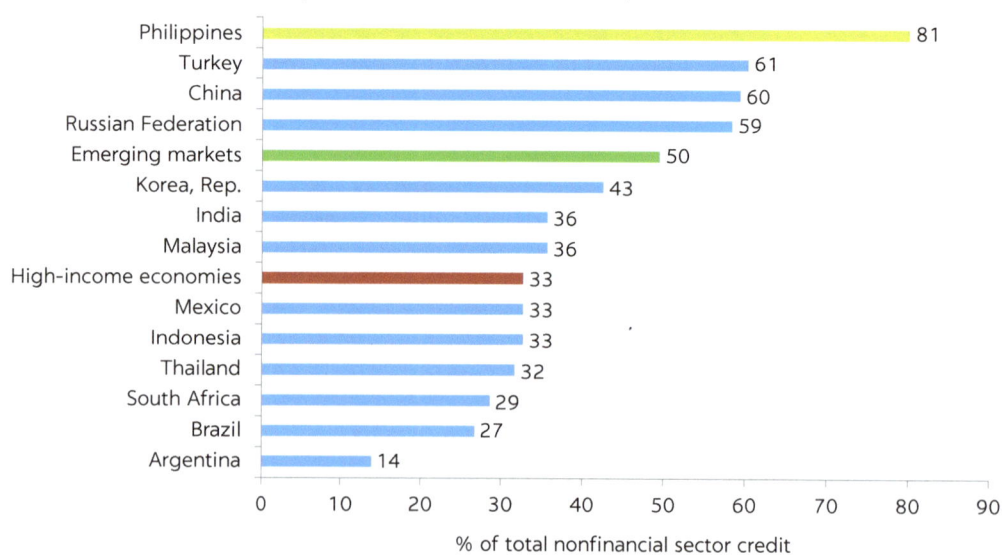

% of total nonfinancial sector credit

Source: Bank for International Settlements and Bangko Sentral ng Pilipinas data.
Note: Bars for high-income economies and emerging markets (which represent aggregate benchmarks) are in different colors to facilitate comparison with the Philippines and other countries.

small and medium firms in ASEAN countries. The Philippines provides small and medium firms with better access to bank credit and microfinance than the median in ASEAN, but less access to alternative sources of enterprise finance than Indonesia, Malaysia, and Thailand.

The high cost of energy aside, the Philippines faces two main infrastructure constraints to increased GVC participation: digital connectivity and physical connectivity. The *World Development Report 2020* identifies the connectivity constraints that countries face as a result of geography (World Bank 2020b). For an archipelago country like the Philippines, the need for trade infrastructure (reform customs, liberalization of transportation services, and investment in ports and roads) and advanced logistics services (investment in multimodal transportation infrastructure) is compounded by digital connectivity challenges (the liberalization of ICT services and investment in basic ICT as well as broadband infrastructure), which are essential for seamless participation in GVCs. These challenges call for sustained public and private investment in connectivity.

The internet in the Philippines needs urgent improvement. The country's 4G/LTE mobile broadband network reaches only 72 percent of the population, the regional average being 82 percent (World Bank 2020a). Only 5 percent of Filipinos have fixed broadband, compared to the regional average of 10 percent. Average mobile download speed is slower, at 26 megabits per second, than the regional average of 34 megabits per second. Average fixed broadband speed is only 38 megabits per second versus the regional average of 92 megabits per second. Furthermore, the populationwide coverage of 4G networks also lags coverage in other countries in the region. These gaps need to be closed for the digital economy to contribute effectively to economic recovery and allow businesses to market their products and services online. Furthermore, improved internet services will be an asset to the BPO sector and will strengthen the participation of the Philippines in the TMT cluster.

Inadequate internet is the result of persistent underinvestment due to insufficient competition, but improvements are happening. The lack of a competition law until 2016 and inability of the regulator, the National Telecommunications Commission, to prevent mergers and acquisitions over the years have resulted in a highly concentrated market, with two dominant players, each controlling and operating its own single, vertically integrated network. Only in 2018 was the government able to announce a plan to accelerate the construction of telecommunications towers by building 50,000 towers by 2022.

Philippine bureaucracy is limited by a range of public administration challenges. According to an assessment conducted in 2019, the most prevalent challenges are overlapping responsibilities and duplication between agencies (World Bank 2019). Numerous legislative gaps prevent collaboration between agencies, requiring companies to visit multiple agencies to comply with requirements. Moreover, many business permits need to be renewed on a frequent (often annual) basis, generating continuing compliance costs as well as repeated opportunities for corruption. Furthermore, business regulations in the Philippines are among the most complex in the world. Indeed, according to the World Bank's 2020 Worldwide Governance Indicators, the Philippines ranks 53.37 out of 100 on regulatory quality and 56.25 on government effectiveness among all countries in the world. In an economy where business regulation is cumbersome or ambiguous, the allocation of resources is distorted by stifling entrepreneurship in favor of maintaining a less optimal status quo. Limited competition in productive sectors and restrictive FDI and trade policies also hinder Filipino firms from innovating and adopting new technologies. Numerous regulations provide protection for incumbent firms, which discourages the entry of new firms and the ability of existing firms to improve productivity. A low level of FDI and trade reduces access to technology and the opportunity to learn more about more sophisticated and contested markets.

Contract enforcement also presents some challenges. In the 2020 Worldwide Governance Indicators for the rule of law, which measure the extent to which agents have confidence in contract enforcement, property rights, and the courts, the Philippines ranks 31.73 out of 100 among all countries in the world. Limited court automation and case management systems mean that courts do not report the time it takes to dispose of a case, do not provide single-case progress reports, and are opaque about the age of pending cases. The heavily overburdened judiciary suffers from significant governance challenges. Judicial inefficiency hampers inclusive growth by favoring established and well-connected firms with the resources to engage in protracted court battles. A poorly functioning judiciary helps to entrench existing oligopolies and discourages the birth and growth of small and medium enterprises.

Data from firms confirm that corruption was widespread. In the World Bank 2015 Enterprise Survey, 35 percent of firms identified corruption as a major constraint, more than double the average among countries in East Asia and Pacific. The fraction of firms reporting that gifts were expected for various government transactions was also high, but in most cases was below the average for other countries in the region. The top reasons for giving gifts were "to get things done" (59 percent), to get a construction permit (40 percent), and to secure a government contract (21 percent). The Worldwide Governance Indicators for control of corruption rank the Philippines 34.13 out of 100 among all countries in 2020, dropping from 39.90 in 2015.

Bureaucracy could be improved by enhancing transparency, predictability, and accountability. The government has made major progress toward overcoming the regulatory burden that restricts trade, competition, and private investment. The enactment of the Ease of Doing Business and Efficient Government Service Delivery Act in 2018 and the implementing rules and regulations in 2019 aimed to ensure that regulations do not add undue regulatory burdens and costs, which restrict trade, competition, and private investment. The operationalization of the Anti-Red Tape Authority to implement this law, which requires shorter processing time for government transactions and greater use of automation to facilitate the applications process, is ongoing through various reform task forces. Between 2019 and 2021, the Anti-Red Tape Authority automatically approved 8,510 licenses and permits. It institutionalized the regulatory impact assessments in policy making to ensure that legal and regulatory issuances are based on precise definitions of the market failure to be resolved, cost-benefit analyses of different regulatory options, and public consultations with affected stakeholders. Accelerating these reforms significantly improves the business environment outside special economic zones and facilitates the participation of domestic suppliers in targeted GVCs. According to key stakeholders in the IMT, TMT, and HLS clusters who took part in a roundtable organized as part of this study, streamlining permits and licenses is urgently needed in the logistics sector (permit requirements for trucks, freight forwarding), the telecommunications sector (poles and ducts for fiber rollout), and the central business portal (automated application for registering a business). In alignment with these priority areas, the Red Tape Authority undertook an interagency program to reduce permitting requirements in the connectivity sector from 241 to 16 days, in the logistics sector from 271 to 35 days, and in the food and pharmaceutical sector from 63 to 21 days.

NOTES

1. A flood in Thailand (Taglioni and Winkler 2016) and an earthquake in Japan (Todo, Kentaro, and Matous 2014).
2. Joint Administrative Order no. 20-01.
3. To date, the Philippines has signed free trade agreements with Japan and European states (Iceland, Liechtenstein, Norway, Switzerland); an agreement with the Republic of Korea is being signed soon. This number is quite low relative to the Philippines' neighbors, which have free trade agreements with strategic markets such as Canada, the European Union, India, or the United States.
4. See https://newsbytes.ph/2020/07/27/boom-in-animation-virtual-production-seen-in-ph-amid-pandemic/.

REFERENCES

A. T. Kearney. 2019. "Racing toward the Future: Artificial Intelligence in Southeast Asia." Kearney, Chicago, IL. https://www.kearney.com/digital/article/?/a/racing-toward-the-future-artificial-intelligence-in-southeast-asia.

Baldwin, Richard, and Beatrice Weder di Mauro. 2020. *Economics in the Time of COVID-19.* London: Centre for Economic Policy Research.

Boehm, Christoph, Aaron Flaaen, and Nitya Pandalai-Nayar. 2019. "Input Linkages and the Transmission of Shocks: Firm-Level Evidence from the 2011 Tōhoku Earthquake." *Review of Economics and Statistics* 101 (1): 60–75.

Cirera, Xavier, Andrew D. Mason, Francesca de Nicola, Smita Kuriakose, Davide S. Mare, and Trang Thu Tran. 2021. *The Innovation Imperative for Developing East Asia.* World Bank East Asia and Pacific Regional Report. Washington, DC: World Bank.

Deloitte. 2018. *2017 Semi-Deloitte Workforce Survey.* London: Deloitte. https://www.semi.org/en/workforce-development/diversity-programs/deloitte-study.

Grundke, Robert, Stéphanie Jamet, Margarita Kalamova, François Keslair, and Mariagrazia Squicciarini. 2017. "Skills and Global Value Chains: A Characterization." OECD Publishing, Paris.

Hunt, Will, and Remco Zwetsloot. 2020. "The Chipmakers: U.S. Strength and Priorities for the High-End Semiconductor Workforce." CSET Issue Brief, Center for Security and Emerging Technology, Georgetown University, Washington, DC.

Jaimovich, Nir, and Henry E. Siu. 2020. "Job Polarization and Jobless Recoveries." *Review of Economics and Statistics* 102 (1): 129–47.

LinkedIn. 2020. "Emerging Jobs Report Philippines." LinkedIn, Mountain View, CA. https://business.linkedin.com/content/dam/me/business/en-us/talent-solutions/emerging-jobs-report/Linkedin_EJR_PH_final.pdf.

OECD (Organisation for Economic Co-operation and Development). 2015. "New Approaches to SME and Entrepreneurship Financing: Broadening the Range of Instruments." OECD, Paris.

OECD (Organisation for Economic Co-operation and Development). 2018. "Access to Finance in SME Policy Index: ASEAN 2018: Boosting Competitiveness and Inclusive Growth." Economic Research Institute for ASEAN and East Asia, OECD, Paris.

Qiang, Christine Zhenwei, Yan Liu, and Victor Steenbergen. 2021. *An Investment Perspective on Global Value Chains.* Washington, DC: World Bank.

Taglioni, Daria, and Deborah Winkler. 2016. "Making Global Value Chains Work for Development." World Bank, Washington, DC.

Todo, Yasuyuki, Nakajima Kentaro, and Petr Matous. 2014. "Firm-Level Simulation of Supply Chain Disruption Triggered by Actual and Predicted Earthquakes." *Journal of Regional Science* 55 (2): 209–29.

U-ACT (Universal Access to Competitiveness and Trade). 2009. "Assessment of Training Policies of CHED, TESDA, and Industry to Address Employment Mismatch." U-ACT, Metro Manila.

UNCTAD (United Nations Conference on Trade and Development). 2021. *Global Investment Trends Monitor Report 2021.* Geneva: UNCTAD.

WEF (World Economic Forum). 2019a. "ASEAN Youth: Technology, Skills and the Future of Work." WEF, Geneva.

WEF (World Economic Forum). 2019b. *Global Competitiveness Report.* Geneva: WEF.

World Bank. 2018. *World Development Report 2018: Learning to Realize Education's Promise.* Washington, DC: World Bank.

World Bank. 2019. "Systematic Country Diagnostic of the Philippines: Realizing the Filipino Dream for 2040." World Bank, Washington, DC.

World Bank. 2020a. *Philippines Digital Economy Report 2020: A Better Normal under COVID-19; Digitalizing the Philippine Economy Now.* Washington, DC: World Bank.

World Bank. 2020b. *World Development Report 2020: Trading for Development in the Age of Global Value Chains.* Washington, DC: World Bank.

4 Policies to Foster GVC Participation

The *World Development Report 2020* is useful for understanding the role of the Philippines in the industrial, manufacturing, and transportation (IMT); technology, media, and telecommunication (TMT); and health and life sciences (HLS) clusters. Participation in global value chains (GVCs) is determined by fundamentals such as factor endowments, market size, geography, and institutional quality, differentiated by the level of development of each country (World Bank 2020b). These fundamentals can be grouped as institutions, infrastructure, and interventions. Institutions refer to cross-cutting policies and institutional reforms that could foster the Philippines' participation in the targeted clusters.[1] Infrastructure refers to connectivity infrastructure. Interventions refer to the targeted provision of infrastructure and services in special economic zones, upgrading strategies, and incentives, such as the Corporate Recovery and Tax Incentives for Enterprise (CREATE) Act, that could foster participation in the three targeted clusters. Choosing the right policies can shape each one of these fundamental areas and thus the Philippines' participation in the IMT, TMT, and HLS clusters.

This chapter explores ways to mobilize key stakeholders (government, lead firms, and domestic suppliers) as the country moves toward a post-COVID-19 recovery that maximizes job creation,[2] attracts foreign direct investment (FDI), and maximizes export revenue. Table 4.1 summarizes proposed high-priority cross-cutting and cluster-specific policy actions.

INSTITUTIONS

The Philippines has many policy and institutional constraints, but three must be addressed in the short term to increase the country's participation in the IMT, TMT, and HLS clusters. These constraints are related to attractiveness to FDI, access to skills, and access to finance.

FDI attractiveness policies

To address FDI constraints, the Philippine Senate is examining legislation amending three laws: the Foreign Investments Act, the Retail Trade

TABLE 4.1 **Summary of high-priority cross-cutting and sector-specific policy actions for the Philippines**

POLICY AREA	CONSTRAINTS	INSTITUTIONS CROSS-CUTTING POLICIES AND INSTITUTIONAL REFORMS	INFRASTRUCTURE POLICIES TO ADDRESS CONNECTIVITY CONSTRAINTS	INTERVENTIONS POLICIES TO FOSTER PARTICIPATION IN THE THREE CLUSTERS[a]
Trade	• Overheads and bottlenecks associated with exporting, which have resulted in the largest contraction of exports in 40 years, despite a narrowing of the monthly trade imbalance to US$2.3 billion in February 2021	• Implement tariff commitments and harmonize rules of origin with RCEP members • Consider establishing preferential trade agreements with strategic trade partners to attract FDI in key clusters	• Fully implement the Customs Modernization and Tariff Act by establishing a national single window to facilitate trade and improve the overall competitiveness of the economy	
	• Propensity of pharmaceutical companies to serve regional markets rather than to export due to high trade costs, practicality, and profitability	• Enable domestic pharmaceutical companies to obtain US Food and Drug Administration approval		
Foreign direct investment	• Lack of investor confidence • Loss of competitiveness vis-à-vis competing locations (for example, Vietnam) • Inability of foreign investors to engage international trainers and mentors • Highest power costs in the region, with the exception of Japan • Investment promotion that was ill-equipped to attract the next generation of foreign investors • Growing concern of investors about the lack of policy on how the government wants industry to look by 2030	• Fully implement amendments to the Foreign Investments Act, the Retail Trade Liberalization Act, and the Public Service Act to boost FDI attractiveness in key sectors • Fully implement the CREATE Act through the immediate issuance of the Strategic Investments Priorities Plan • Reintroduce and adopt a Philippine sovereign wealth fund act		

continued

TABLE 4.1, *continued*

POLICY AREA	CONSTRAINTS	INSTITUTIONS CROSS-CUTTING POLICIES AND INSTITUTIONAL REFORMS	INFRASTRUCTURE POLICIES TO ADDRESS CONNECTIVITY CONSTRAINTS	INTERVENTIONS POLICIES TO FOSTER PARTICIPATION IN THE THREE CLUSTERS[a]
	• Overdependence on imported inputs and raw materials • Inadequate contingency planning for investors supplying international customers just in time • Opacity of electric vehicle and associated infrastructure policy and timelines, dissuading investors from making medium- to long-term commitments • Dependence of the EMS segment on intermediary products and "sunset" products nearing the end of their commercial life cycle • Lack of a biopharmaceutical and life sciences ecosystem • Insufficient investment in telecommunications infrastructure that undermines digitalization • Slow pace of transitioning the BPO segment from cost saving to value addition		• Increase funding for telecommunications infrastructure within the infrastructure investment program via public-private partnerships and sovereign wealth funds	• Promote targeted investment: – Attract tier-two and tier-three suppliers to expand the base of suppliers for aeronautics and diversify from aircraft interiors – Leverage electronics strengths by enabling EMS companies to transition into electric vehicle assembly, component manufacture, and charging infrastructure – Develop the Philippines as a center of excellence for semiconductor design – Leverage the success of global shared services centers to attract investment in IT outsourcing and knowledge process outsourcing – Motivate multinational pharmaceutical companies in the Philippines to outsource contract manufacturing to local companies

continued

TABLE 4.1, *continued*

POLICY AREA	CONSTRAINTS	INSTITUTIONS CROSS-CUTTING POLICIES AND INSTITUTIONAL REFORMS	INFRASTRUCTURE POLICIES TO ADDRESS CONNECTIVITY CONSTRAINTS	INTERVENTIONS POLICIES TO FOSTER PARTICIPATION IN THE THREE CLUSTERS[a]
Skills	• Insufficient skills upgrading within the services sector • Lack of workers with skills required by innovation firms, with about 80% of respondents citing lack of commitment and poor communication and technical skills as impediments	• Amend profession-specific laws to encourage FDI and attract skilled workers in targeted segments (that is, remove "practice of professions" from the Foreign Investments Act and the foreign investment negative list and amend applicable sector or professional regulations) • Simplify work permits and visas to maximize labor mobility and skills provision • Conclude mutual recognition arrangements on professional services in the RCEP to liberalize professional mobility • Fully operationalize the Philippine Qualifications Framework to harmonize and facilitate seamless progression from different levels of education and training, promote skills upgrading and lifelong learning, and be on par with international standards	• Assess the country's internet infrastructure (quality and reliability of internet connection) and expand it to support training programs effectively	• Strengthen industry-academia links to bridge the gaps in workforce capacity building and skills development
	• Very high staff attrition rates within BPO segment before COVID-19 • Within ICT and financial services, shortage of skills and low backward participation in GVCs • Insufficient recognition within the Department of Trade and Industry's AI Road Map that the uptake of AI is slower than in competing countries • Scarcity of workers with advanced skills to support scalability	• Fast-track implementation of the AI Road Map • Conduct a technical skills gap analysis to provide concrete recommendations for reskilling and retooling policies for the three clusters • Expand the provision of and access to online ICT-related education and training courses and the Commission on Higher Education's Service Management (Advanced) Program for BPO centers		• Increase the supply of engineering skills with appropriate (sector-specific) certification • Ensure that the CREATE Act motivates the private sector to upskill personnel through training grants • Develop sectoral skills policy frameworks that are responsive to fast-changing requirements aligned with global standards • Support sector-specific online job fairs

continued

TABLE 4.1, *continued*

| POLICY AREA | CONSTRAINTS | INSTITUTIONS | INFRASTRUCTURE | INTERVENTIONS |
		CROSS-CUTTING POLICIES AND INSTITUTIONAL REFORMS	POLICIES TO ADDRESS CONNECTIVITY CONSTRAINTS	POLICIES TO FOSTER PARTICIPATION IN THE THREE CLUSTERS[a]
GVC integration	• Low productivity of small and medium firms compared with larger firms • Difficulty meeting international quality standards • Difficulty accessing markets • High costs to serve the domestic market given the country's archipelagic state • Inadequacies in business operation, such as lack of proper facilities and access to relevant technologies • Fragmentation of full support services to small and medium enterprises • Large gaps in the entrepreneurial ecosystem	• Prioritize the adoption and adaptation of existing new technologies over R&D to improve the access of small and medium enterprises to new technology • Address constraints on small and medium enterprises in accessing finance, such as the ineffective public credit guarantee scheme for small and medium firms and inefficient insolvency regimes • Complete an entrepreneurship ecosystem audit to promote an innovation ecosystem in cities and special economic zones hosting targeted segments • Conduct reverse trade fairs for multinational corporations located in the Philippines to source more inputs locally		
	• Reluctance of small and medium enterprises to engage with multinational corporations wanting to source locally			• Attract tier-one and tier-two suppliers to create greater opportunities for GVC integration by local small and medium enterprises
Sector competitiveness	• Gaps in the range and quality of services, which undermines manufacturing performance and market accessibility • Risk aversion of local conglomerates, which are more interested in trading than in manufacturing and are content to serve the domestic market	• Formulate and endorse a policy statement on the IMT cluster to boost investor confidence • Develop and strengthen cluster dynamics to increase the services content of goods	• Continue to implement the Common Tower Policy to increase private investment in ICT • Adopt and implement the Open Access in Data Transmission Act to promote the digital economy	

continued

TABLE 4.1, *continued*

POLICY AREA	CONSTRAINTS	INSTITUTIONS CROSS-CUTTING POLICIES AND INSTITUTIONAL REFORMS	INFRASTRUCTURE POLICIES TO ADDRESS CONNECTIVITY CONSTRAINTS	INTERVENTIONS POLICIES TO FOSTER PARTICIPATION IN THE THREE CLUSTERS[a]
	• Inability of productivity and innovation spillovers from FDI and domestic multinational corporations to sustain improved competitiveness • Need for a new, more export-oriented electric vehicle model to develop the automotive sector, as the CARS Program has not achieved the desired impact • For electronics, a positive but modest trade balance and exceptionally low value added, with food processing, for example, generating twice the value added as electronics • An embryonic biopharmaceutical and life sciences sector that lacks a core, a champion, and a cluster culture • Overdependence of aerospace exports on Airbus and Boeing; insufficient focus on supplying leading aerospace companies in the Asia Pacific region and in China • Lag in BPO and IT-enabled services with regard to IT outsourcing, knowledge process outsourcing, and capitalizing on surges in health care BPO centers	• Within the IMT cluster policy, articulate the following: – How the aerospace, automobile, and electronics industry will look by 2030 – Parameters of a core electric vehicle policy, including when all new vehicles sold must be electric or hybrid, a charging infrastructure for electric vehicles, and a time frame for monetization – An electronics policy elaborating how the Philippines will emerge as a center of excellence for semiconductor design and electric vehicle electronics – A policy and strategic direction for converting the Philippines' natural resources in quartz and copper oxide into lithium-ion batteries for electric vehicles and copper for electric vehicle motors • Align TMT policy with the AI Road Map – Unlock the GVC efficiency gains of the verticals (sectors) being supported by BPO centers – Continue decreasing "Manila-centricity" for BPO centers to the extent that the business case will allow • Fill the HLS policy vacuum by elevating the Philippine Pharma Road Map under preparation to an HLS policy: – Accelerate development of the life science and biotechnology cluster by developing (a) a knowledge center of excellence, (b) an innovation ecosystem, and (c) a superior enabling environment with, for example, a dedicated technology park or campus and venture capital provision – Ensure that the Philippine Food and Drug Administration can streamline and accelerate a new drug-approval process, while resolving the lack of bioequivalence exposure within the Philippines	• Leverage the country's strengths in electronics to design, build, and export electric vehicle charging infrastructure	• Conduct a GVC reconfiguration analysis of companies to support stronger cluster links • Develop a five-year plan to develop and upgrade GVCs in the three clusters

Source: World Bank staff.
Note: Color code: light blue = economy wide, light green = cluster specific. AI = artificial intelligence; BPO = business process outsourcing; CARS = Comprehensive Automotive Resurgence Strategy; CREATE = Corporate Recovery and Tax Incentives for Enterprises; EMS = electronics manufacturing services; FDI = foreign direct investment; GVC = global value chain; HLS = health and life sciences; ICT = information and communication technology; IMT = industrial, manufacturing, and transportation; IT = information technology; R&D = research and development; RCEP = Regional Comprehensive Economic Partnership; TMT = technology, media, and telecommunication.
a. Including targeted infrastructure and upgrading of investor-trader service provision.

Liberalization Act, and the Public Service Act (Government of the Philippines, 1936, 1991, and 2000). Two proposed amendments to the 1991 Foreign Investments Act would remove the "practice of professions" from the foreign investment negative list and reduce mandatory direct local hires by foreign investors. Box 4.1 describes similar reforms undertaken in Indonesia, which, before the reforms, was second only to the Philippines in terms of tight regulatory restrictions on foreign investment. This change is expected to attract more skilled foreign professionals, so that Filipinos can gain new knowledge and broaden their existing skills. Amendments to the 2000 Retail Trade Liberalization Act include facilitating retail e-commerce, reducing the minimum paid-up capital requirement, retaining the reciprocity requirement, and removing the prequalification requirement. Amendments to the Public Service Act aim to limit public utilities to sectors engaged in the distribution and transmission of electricity as well as the distribution of water or sewerage systems, which are constitutionally subject to a cap of 40 percent foreign ownership.[3] The amendments will lift the restrictions on foreign equity, particularly on telecommunications and transportation service providers. Timely adoption of these amendments and their implementing rules and regulations is essential for the Philippines to take advantage of increased opportunities to upgrade and participate in the IMT, TMT, and HLS clusters.

BOX 4.1

Investment reform in Indonesia

Indonesia attracts less foreign direct investment (FDI) relative to gross domestic product (GDP) than its regional peers, consistent with Indonesia's tight regulatory restrictions on FDI. In a survey by the Organisation for Economic Co-operation and Development, conducted in 2018 before the recent reforms, Indonesia was the third most restrictive country surveyed. In the region, only the Philippines was more restrictive (figure B4.1.1).

Indonesia's negative investment list places different types of restrictions on investments, particularly limits on foreign equity. The list applies at least one restriction in 28 percent of all economic sectors and either limits foreign equity participation or prohibits foreign investment altogether in 20 percent. Examples include horticultural production, ports, power plants with capacity below 1 megawatt, and supermarkets smaller than 1,200 square meters. In addition, the list reserves many agricultural, industrial, and service subsectors exclusively for small and medium enterprises, effectively barring foreign investors from operating such firms in Indonesia.

Investment restrictions deter the entry of foreign firms, particularly export-oriented ones, which is crucial to linking the Indonesian economy with global value chains and increasing its competitiveness. Export-oriented manufacturing FDI is associated with rapid growth of labor productivity, higher average wages, introduction of more new products, and higher investment rates. Limiting the entry of foreign firms stifles technological spillovers and competition, translating into lower productivity and exports both in the sectors exposed to the restrictions and in downstream sectors.

To open more sectors to private investment, particularly FDI, Indonesia recently reduced the number of business activities subject to at least one investment restriction from 813 to 260, as evidenced by Presidential Regulation no. 10/2021. The reform fully opened many sectors where FDI was not allowed or was permitted only with a minority shareholding (that is, it allowed up to 100 percent foreign equity). Examples of such sectors include fishing, horticulture, small and medium supermarkets, ports, airports, shipping, mobile and fixed telecommunications services, power plant generation and distribution, and auto repair services. The bulk of the activities that are still subject to restrictions

continued

BOX 4.1, *continued*

FIGURE B4.1.1

Regulatory restrictions on foreign direct investment, by country, 2018

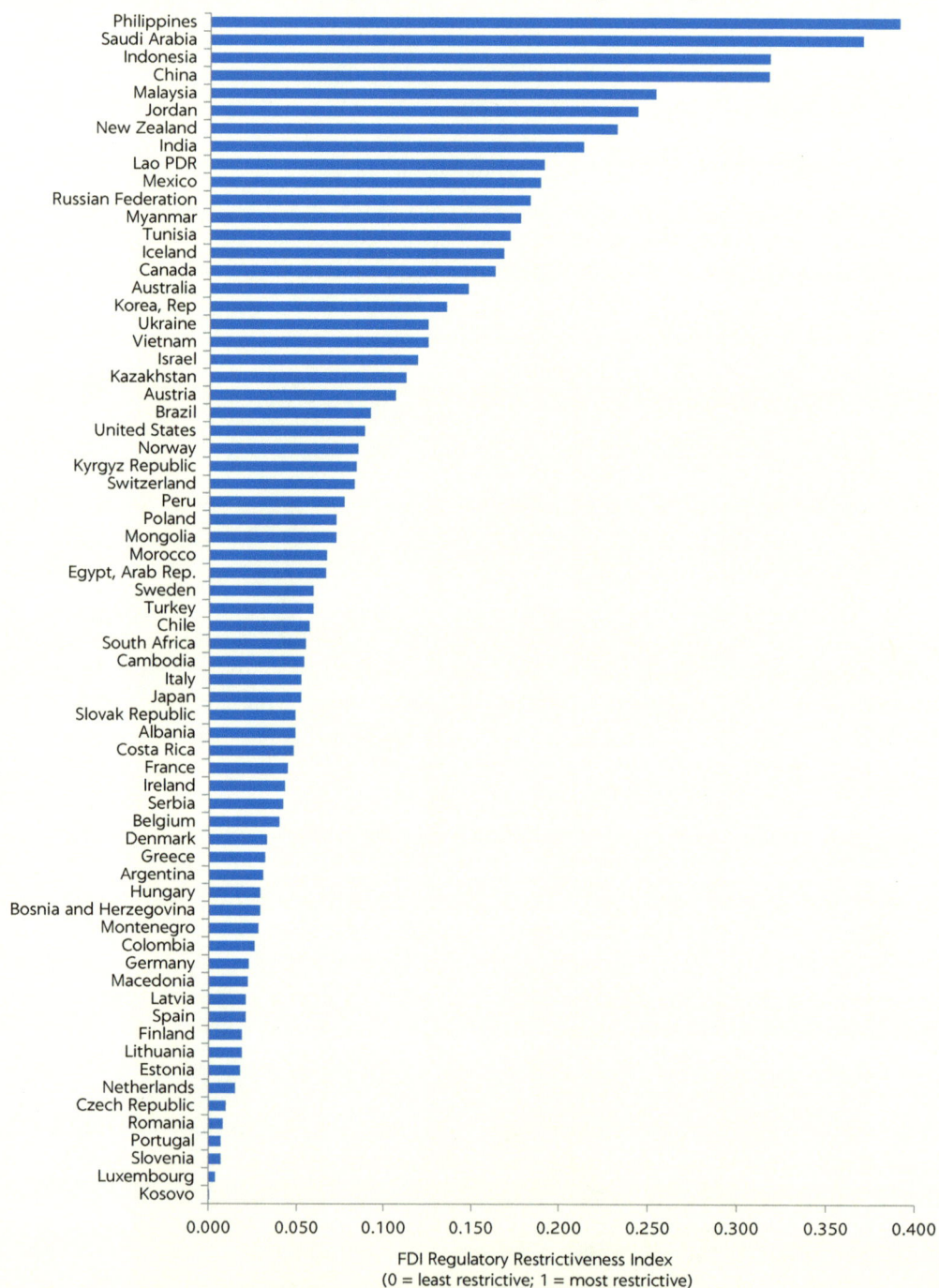

FDI Regulatory Restrictiveness Index
(0 = least restrictive; 1 = most restrictive)

Source: Organisation for Economic Co-operation and Development (OECD) data.
Note: FDI = foreign direct investment.

continued

BOX 4.1, *continued*

include (a) relatively small activities, which are reserved for small and medium enterprises or have to be undertaken in partnership with them, and (b) sectors considered of public interest, which require minority or no foreign ownership.

The removal of investment restrictions is expected to generate between US$4.1 billion and US$6 billion in additional investments, both foreign and domestic, in the liberalized sectors, which translates into an estimated increase in GDP growth of between 0.12 and 0.17 percentage point, close to the estimated GDP growth of 0.2 percent per year from liberalization across all sectors. Eliminating all limits on foreign equity across all sectors could increase FDI by US$3.8 billion per year and domestic investment by US$3.1 billion per year (Calì et al. 2020). The increased investment and embedded technology and know-how would help to increase potential output and counter the negative impact of the COVID-19 crisis, increasing growth by as much as 0.2 percent per year.

Source: Prepared by Angella Faith Montfaucon.

As a result of these reforms, Indonesia now has one of the most open FDI regulatory regimes in the region. Investors are increasingly searching for new bases of production as global value chains are reconfiguring. In turn, investment flows are expected to raise productivity, employment, and wages, bringing lower prices and better products and services for consumers. Although these reforms have addressed many of Indonesia's upstream restrictions on investments, more could be done to address remaining barriers, including reducing and eventually eliminating the list of sectors reserved for small and medium enterprises and turning burdensome minimum local content requirements across various sectors into positive incentives to use local suppliers. In addition, these upstream activities could be complemented by downstream activities, for example, enhancing investment promotion and addressing investors' grievances more effectively, which could improve the retention of investments.

Proposed amendments to the Foreign Investments Act are a move in the right direction, but adjustments might be needed as new challenges surface. Excluding a profession from the scope of the Foreign Investments Act implies that it will not be part of the foreign investment negative list. However, being excluded from the act does not automatically imply liberalization. It only means that the practice of a profession by qualified foreign professionals and foreign equity participation in a firm directly engaged in corporate practice by qualified foreign professionals will be governed by the applicable laws, rules, regulations, and other international agreements between the Philippines and other countries. Furthermore, the liberalization of FDI in professional services generally has only a limited effect and must be accompanied by mode 4 (immigration) liberalization. While establishment rights are valuable, without simultaneous liberalization of the movement of people, foreign investors may be hesitant to engage. The temporary movement of foreign employees is also key to facilitating knowledge transfer and skills upgrading.

Alternative reforms could be considered to liberalize professional services. First, profession-specific laws could be amended to allow FDI in specific professions that are of strategic importance. Second, national treatment could be established in the Foreign Investments Act to provide deeper liberalization. Mode 4 liberalization should be supported by addressing restrictions on visas, work permits, and qualifications. In addition, consideration should be given to removing Part A of the foreign investment negative list, known as the Annex on Professions, which governs mode 4 provision of professional services. Part A is inconsistent with the Foreign Investments Act, which is concerned with mode 3 (FDI). To ensure transparency for foreign investors, it should be restated in another instrument.

Policies for advanced skills

The Philippines can take advantage of ongoing reconfiguration in the IMT, TMT, and HLS clusters to address structural skills constraints. To do so, the following actions are needed:

- Amend profession-specific laws to encourage FDI and attract skills in targeted segments (that is, remove the "practice of professions" in the Foreign Investments Act and in the foreign investment negative list and amend applicable sector and professional regulations).
- Simplify work permits and visas to maximize labor mobility and skills provision.
- Pursue mutual recognition arrangements on professional services in the Regional Comprehensive Economic Partnership to liberalize professional mobility.
- Fully operationalize the Philippine Qualifications Framework to harmonize and facilitate seamless progression between levels of education and training qualifications, promote skills upgrading and lifelong learning, and meet international standards in this area.

To boost advanced skills, the government needs to accelerate its innovation strategy. In 2019, the Philippine Innovation Act (Republic Act no. 11293) was approved to support education, training, and research and development (R&D) to foster innovation, internationalization, and digitalization and to promote sustainable and inclusive growth. The implementation rules and regulations were published in February 2020. Accelerating the implementation of this strategy could help to create a Silicon Valley type of environment in which cities and clusters of cities host engineers, technicians, doctors, and nurses working in the IMT, TMT, and HLS clusters. Such an environment would encourage the circulation of knowledge. For instance, an excellent electronics hub in Cebu-Mactan is connected to the auto and aerospace sectors, with key companies such as Analog Devices and Surface Technologies. Another example is Baguio in Central Luzon, which hosts Moog Controls and Texas Instruments, two strategic lead firms. Helping analog firms to acquire digital skills and to digitize could help these firms to connect and integrate with global GVCs.

The Philippines would benefit from an innovation strategy that prioritizes adoption and adaptation. The Philippines ranked 86 out of 137 on the 2019 Global Entrepreneurship Index and is lagging behind its Association of Southeast Asian Nations neighbors in the following areas: company spending on R&D, collaboration between universities and industry on R&D, foreign direct investment, and technology transfer. Poor connectivity between public research institutions and the private sector, along with the limited productivity and poor extension services of firms, leads to a dearth of knowledge capital. Given these constraints, firms would benefit from policies supporting the adoption and adaptation of existing knowledge and technologies and boosting relevant innovation capabilities.

Access to finance

Capital market development in the Philippines is restricted by the conglomerate structure of the economy. According to a recent report, only 30 percent of firms have a bank loan or line of credit (World Bank 2020a). COVID-19 has worsened firms' access to credit, not only because credit bureau data are lacking but also because the information traditionally collected by credit bureaus (payment performance on credits granted) is not available or is inadequate to perform a robust analysis of creditworthiness. Other constraints include overreliance by lenders on immovables collateral, an ineffective public credit guarantee scheme for small and medium enterprises, inefficient insolvency regimes, fragmented institutional setup of financial regulators, and limited supervisory power. Addressing these constraints is a prerequisite to fostering the participation of domestic firms in strategic GVCs through various forms of financing.

Given the state of the country's stock exchanges, the prospects of an initial public offering are limited. Reforms to increase access to equity financing for small and medium enterprises could boost the country's participation in targeted GVCs by attracting strategic partners willing to provide risk capital to young, innovative domestic firms. For instance, collective investment schemes could support the development of equity financing.[4] Given that the dominant banking sector has high liquidity that crowds out other forms of private financial intermediation, government intervention to facilitate the mobilization of domestic saving through collective investment schemes is critical.

Reforms to equity financing could help domestic small and medium enterprises to participate in strategic GVCs. In the Association of Southeast Asian Nations, the bulk of private equity and venture capital deals take place in Singapore, with Indonesia and Malaysia vying for second place. In the top five destinations, including Thailand and Vietnam, these funds ranged from US$3.7 billion in Singapore to US$72 million in Thailand in 2015. The amount of funding for these deals rose in Thailand and Vietnam in 2016, but dropped in Indonesia, Malaysia, and Singapore (AVCJ 2017). The majority of these deals are in the TMT cluster (Bhalla et al. 2012; Preqin 2017). A trade sale is the most common form of exit, followed by an initial public offering (AVCJ 2017), as is the case in many Organisation for Economic Co-operation and Development markets.

Three key initiatives could improve capital markets, attracting issuers and investors (see, for example, IMF 2020). The first is to improve investor confidence—for example, by strengthening the quality of supervision and enforcement for market intermediaries and market operators. The second is to expand and deepen the base of investors, both domestic and international. The Philippines lags regional peers in terms of the assets managed by mutual and pension funds and the total assets of insurance companies in proportion to gross domestic product. Current discussions of reforming the public pension fund are a step in the right direction. Creating a level playing field by eliminating regulatory and tax arbitrage among collective investment schemes would be a significant step. Equally important, the pension funds sector could be developed as an institutional investor. State-owned pension funds currently operate on a defined-benefit basis and remain unfunded. The focus should be on developing private pension funds under appropriate regulation. The third is to rationalize the tax regime. The current regime distorts capital market pricing and deters issuance. This situation compares unfavorably with regional peers.[5] Finally, a comprehensive tax reform bill to simplify passive income and financial intermediary taxes is pending in the Senate after passing the House of Representatives.[6] It has some provisions that would improve access to finance for small and medium enterprises.

INFRASTRUCTURE

In addition to the cost of energy,[7] digital connectivity and physical connectivity are major constraints to increased GVC participation. The *World Development Report 2020* looks at the infrastructure challenges to GVC participation in the context of geographic connectivity constraints (World Bank 2020b). For an archipelago country like the Philippines, deficiencies in trade infrastructure and logistics are compounded by poor digital connectivity. All three elements are essential for seamless participation in the global economy, which calls for sustained public and private investment in connectivity.

Ongoing digitalization of the economy means that data and information reform is needed in the Philippines. The use of the internet for selling goods and services is the least extensive in the region, despite companies having comparable information and communication technology (Baller, Dutta, and Lanvin 2016). The COVID-19 pandemic is accelerating the transition to digital, with more work from home, remote education, fintech, e-government, and telemedicine. Recent reforms in the payment system laid the foundation for a rapid increase in digital payments (National Payment Systems Act of 2018 and the New Central Bank Act of 2019) and are underpinning the Philippine Central Bank's Digital Payments Transformation Road Map. With social distancing, quarantines, lockdowns, and fewer mass gatherings becoming the new normal, enhancing the country's digital infrastructure should be a national priority. The proposed Open Access in Data Transmission Act will spur the development of new information and communication technology infrastructure that is essential for a successful digital economy. The act seeks to lower barriers to market entry, fast-track and lower the cost of deploying broadband facilities, and make more bandwidth available for internet services. Executive Order 127, which expands the provision of internet services through inclusive access to satellite services, is also expected to bridge the digital divide by enabling the deployment of infrastructure for underserved areas. To maximize the use of satellite technology, complementary policies (either through legislation or through executive action) and an effective spectrum management policy are needed to address digital literacy and improve access and connectivity.

The IT and Business Process Association sees advantages in the digital economy for enhanced participation in the IMT, TMT, and HLS clusters. The information technology and business process management sector has progressed from pioneer firms in the 1980s, to multinational shared services, to call centers, and to new subsectors. Indeed, Analog Devices, Canon, Fairchild, Kyocera, Lexmark, Maxim, Murata, On Semiconductor, Ricoh, Schneider, Toshiba, and Tsukiden are electronics companies that set up in the Philippines and later helped to establish the business process outsourcing sector. The semiconductor sector remains the backbone of Philippine participation in the IMT cluster. Pharmaceuticals, medical devices, and health care services are becoming more integrated. As a result, the management of information is becoming more important in the HLS cluster as well. The development of the TMT cluster in the Philippines could facilitate the emergence of an HLS cluster, with the IMT cluster reaching the medical device sector, the TMT cluster reaching the health care services sector, and the pharmaceutical sector attracting investment in lead firms while promoting networks of domestic suppliers.

The Bureau of Customs and the Bureau of Internal Revenue have prioritized the digitalization of their processes, placing e-government, and thus the TMT cluster, at the center of the country's competitiveness. The Bureau of Customs began upgrading its processing systems in 2018. The COVID-19 pandemic has shown the need to improve trade-related procedures, which has motivated policy makers to speed up reforms. Pandemic lockdowns led the Bureau of Customs to fast-track the immediate adoption of emergency protocols, such as online filing, processing of incomplete applications, acceptance of digital payments, and creation of a one-stop clearinghouse for medical supplies. This effort was expanded to include other transactions, such as payments for cargo handling, storage, and transportation scheduling. This automation will strengthen accountability, eliminate a significant number of face-to-face interactions, reduce delays, and minimize discretionary action by officials. The Bureau of Internal Revenue also instituted its Digital Transformation Road Map in 2019 and has sought to partner with agencies that are more advanced on digitalization, such as the Australian Tax Office and the Russian Federal Tax Service, to learn from their journey in implementing e-invoicing. Timely implementation of this road map will significantly improve the business environment.

The COVID-19 crisis has also provided an opportunity to accelerate the implementation of some infrastructure projects designed to ease connectivity and mobility. The Metro Rail Transit Line 3 in the National Capital Region is now more reliable and faster, with 23 trains running at up to 60 kilometers per hour, compared to 10 trains running at 30 kilometers per hour, while the east extension of the Light Rail Transit Line 2 has reduced travel time between Manila and Antipolo to just 40 minutes from between two and three hours in the past. Further, the Skyway Stage 3 has helped to decongest Epifanio de los Santos Avenue (EDSA) and other major roads in Metro Manila through a partnership with the private sector. Phase 1 of the North-South Commuter Railway, which will connect Malolos, Bulacan, to Tutuban, Manila, is set to be completed in 2022 (Gines 2021). Other projects related to easing traffic and facilitating the flow of goods include the EDSA Busway Project, the Taguig Integrated Terminal Exchange, and the North Integrated Terminal Exchange. Since July 2016, the Department of Transportation has completed 233 airport projects nationwide, 19 of which were inaugurated in 2021. Likewise, 111 seaport projects have been completed, while 62 projects are out for procurement. The Department of Information and Communications Technology has also outlined measures designed to improve the Philippines' digital readiness, with a plan to install 5,000 towers each year over the next three years. This effort is expected to increase investments in the telecommunications sector, particularly for major telecommunications companies like DITO Telecommunity, Globe Telecom, and PLDT. The Department of Information and Communications Technology also has programs to improve connectivity in Mindanao and Visayas, especially the Free Wi-Fi for All Program in public places nationwide and in geographically isolated and disadvantaged areas.

Scaling up such positive developments in physical connectivity will boost the growth of exports in regional hubs. This effort could use physical connectivity to reprioritize the official Build, Build, Build Program in Calabarzon, Cebu, Central Luzon, and National Capital Region, where most of the firms in the IMT, TMT, and HLS clusters are based. This effort should be complemented by the development of advanced logistics and information and communication technology services in these regions, with full implementation of the Customs Modernization and Tariff Act. Also needed is an effort to promote competition and streamline the issuance of permits for digital infrastructure provision. A comprehensive financing strategy should be considered to maximize successful implementation of these projects.

INTERVENTIONS

Fundamental to increasing domestic and foreign investments in GVCs in the three clusters is establishing an enabling environment through the right institutions and infrastructure. Because these two policy instruments can take time to deliver, governments often use speedier policy instruments, such as incentives, to attract investment. By altering a project's relative costs and associated risks, these targeted policy actions are meant to influence investment decisions in favor of the host country. Fiscal incentives are the most common type of intervention used by low- and middle-income economies (Tavares-Lehmann et al. 2016). They are meant to give firms cost advantages in the form of tax holidays, tax credits, tax deductions, and investment allowances. Countries have also used proactive policies to upgrade their participation in GVCs. This section focuses on how targeted infrastructure and service provision in special economic zones, along with upgrading, could foster participation in the IMT, TMT, and HLS clusters.

Special economic zones

The Philippines is in the process of recalibrating its incentives regime with the Corporate Recovery and Tax Incentives for Enterprise (CREATE) Act. CREATE seeks to cut the corporate income tax and streamline fiscal incentives. The corporate income tax will be lowered from 30 percent to 25 percent for large corporations and to 20 percent for small and medium enterprises. Businesses whose gross sales fall below ₱3 million will pay value added tax of 1 percent instead of 3 percent. CREATE provides incentives to enterprises based on their projects or activities. The Strategic Investments Priorities Plan contains projects or activities that promote long-term growth and sustainable development. Thus, enterprises undergoing projects or activities identified by the Board of Investments are granted incentives. The first Strategic Investments Priorities Plan is scheduled to be released in January 2022. CREATE also grants longer income tax holidays for businesses outside Metro Manila to encourage economic development and create jobs beyond the capital. Other fiscal incentives include exemption from customs duties on imports of capital equipment, raw materials, or spare parts for the registered project or activity; exemption from value added tax on imports; and zero value added tax on local purchases of goods and services used in the registered project or activity.

Setting up special economic zones can foster investment in the IMT, TMT, and HLS clusters. Clearly identifying these sectors in the investment priority plan is a first step to ensuring government commitment to their growth. A long-term view of priorities is appropriate, given the long time frame associated with large capital investments. Incentives can be given to firms based on the priority zones or activities. For instance, Thailand is promoting automotive parts, smart electronics, aircraft and logistics, and medical services along its Eastern Economic Corridor. Firms receive additional exemptions on their corporate and personal income taxes on top of the standard incentives. The corridor consists of special industry promotion zones, target industry promotion zones, and industrial areas within the corridor. Another example is MSC Malaysia, a high-technology business district and the R&D center for information technology industries in Malaysia.

The three clusters could also benefit from additional incentives. In Malaysia, for example, R&D, automation, and innovation receive additional fiscal incentives, such as income tax exemption, concessionary tax rates, accelerated allowances, and exemption from import duty and sales tax. Such incentives would encourage all firms to invest in automation and innovation, but would especially benefit firms in the three GVC clusters, which are heavily involved in innovation and automation. Other possible activities are the skills development of personnel, managerial training, and investment in human capital in exchange for tax deductions. CREATE states, "Upon the recommendation of the Fiscal Incentive Review Board, the President can approve a set of incentives with longer periods of availment, if necessary, to attract highly desirable investment that will bring more employment, higher level of skills training, and greater value added to the economy."

Securing access to affordable energy within special economic zones to host IMT, TMT, and HLS clusters should also be considered. The high cost of energy is crippling manufacturing in the Philippines. In the 1990s and early 2000s, the government embarked on energy sector reform, which phased out virtually all energy subsidies. But market liberalization has not led to more affordable electricity, and the government's technology-neutral, least-cost policies have led to the rapid growth of coal-fired power. The development of industrial parks to host some strategic lead firms and domestic suppliers of the three clusters could be an opportunity to promote the development of green energy. Subsidies and other incentives could be used to crowd in private investment in renewable energy and secure affordable access to energy, which would scale up the Philippines' participation in the IMT, TMT, and HLS clusters. For example, institutional investors could be encouraged to support the United Nations Sustainable Development Goals by creating value in infrastructure, renewable energy, and health care. By raising the bar, the government could help to attract investments in affordable energy and other amenities to specific special economic zones. Full implementation of the country's Nationally Determined Contributions under the Paris Agreement signed in April 2021, which pushes for investing in renewables and cutting greenhouse gas emissions by 75 percent, will help to secure access to clean energy for the development of the three strategic clusters.

Cluster-specific policies

Interviews with firms in the IMT, TMT, and HLS clusters provide insights into sector- and cluster-specific reforms. As documented in table 4.1, given the commonalities affecting the competitiveness of aerospace, automotive, and electronics, the next steps for the IMT cluster could be to use the GVC reconfiguration policy dialogue initiated by this study as the fulcrum for an IMT Policy 2030. For the TMT cluster, next steps could focus on motivating and enabling existing business process outsourcing centers to upgrade into big data and analytics and accelerating skills provision to build on the Philippines' shared services center successes in supporting global operations. For the HLS cluster, a policy framework is needed to accelerate the transition of the pharmaceutical industry into a vibrant and innovative biopharmaceutical industry by 2030. This effort could be centered on leveraging US Food and Drug Administration approval to open doors to key export markets. Three prerequisites are essential for a successful biotechnology and life sciences cluster: a knowledge center of excellence, an innovation ecosystem, and a life sciences technology park. Such dedicated zones have led to the development of biotech clusters in Boston, Cambridge, Edinburgh, Munich, San Francisco, and Singapore.

As a follow-up to this study, a more systematic cluster assessment is being framed as a demonstration scheme. It will start with selecting one pilot cluster from the three strategic clusters to deepen the technical assistance. Once a cluster is selected, a pilot[8] cluster competitiveness diagnostic will be conducted with a view to demonstrating the type of outputs that can be achieved through a Competitiveness Reinforcement Initiative (CRI) (figure 4.1). This work will produce several documents that mirror the steps of market discovery and policy creation typically covered in the course of a CRI. The World Bank will work hand in hand with the Philippine government in developing this analysis and tailoring it to the local context in later phases. Based on the experience of countries like Belarus and Croatia, six weeks of capacity building are needed to familiarize key stakeholders with the CRI process. Given budget and time constraints, the team will explore a shorter version of one or two weeks of capacity building as part of the engagement.[9] In addition, the findings will be disseminated to the private sector to validate the diagnostics.[10] Further financial resources and institutional arrangements will be needed—especially in light of COVID-19 restrictions on travel—before commitments are made to conducting a full CRI. However, the pilot will provide useful information, which can be replicated for the other two clusters at a later time (possibly under this same project).

More specifically, the diagnostic will include competitiveness and value chain analysis as well as diagnostics of regulatory impediments in the clusters.

FIGURE 4.1

Phases and work streams of a Competitiveness Reinforcement Initiative

Source: World Bank staff.
Note: M&E = monitoring and evaluation. PM = public meeting.

The results will be used to map essential stakeholders in the value chain and identify competitiveness bottlenecks that deter participation. The overarching research question will examine how firms (in the identified cluster) can compete more effectively in various segments of the market. Data will be gathered through successive steps of the cluster-level diagnostic, which will be split into three outputs in order to mirror the stages of a CRI, serving as an example diagnostic that the client can use to emulate the process in the future.

CONCLUSION

The pandemic has provided the Philippines with a unique opportunity to align policies, the business climate, the pace of reform, and the institutional framework with future challenges. Policies are needed to reverse the Philippines' missed opportunities and strengthen its position in key GVCs. Decisive policy action to ensure that investment is channeled into priority sustainable development sectors has never been so critical. While changing GVC dynamics is beyond the power of most governments, understanding future GVC trends and drivers of change would enable governments to anticipate and respond to changes by realigning existing policies or crafting new policies to maximize the benefits of GVC reconfiguration.

NOTES

1. Cluster-specific interventions will be explored as part of the implementation of these recommendations in a follow-up policy and sectoral dialogue.
2. As discussed in Acemoglu and Restrepo (2019), there may be trade-offs between maximizing export proceeds and jobs, as achieving efficiency and improving productivity may entail automation. This is especially true for IMT, where Industry 4.0 technologies and the digitalization megatrend are predicted to expand the set of tasks that can be performed by machinery and algorithms, replacing labor.
3. Substitute Bill of Senate Bill 2094 filed on September 13, 2021, defines the following activities as being of public utility: distribution of electricity; transmission of electricity; petroleum and petroleum products pipeline transmission systems; petroleum and petroleum products distribution systems; water pipeline distribution systems and wastewater pipeline systems; airports and seaports; and public utility vehicles.
4. A collective investment scheme is any arrangement whereby funds are solicited from the investing public and pooled together for the purpose of investing, reinvesting, or trading in securities or other investment assets or different classes of investments.
5. CREATE, discussed later in this chapter, aims to address some of these distortions.
6. See https://taxreform.dof.gov.ph/tax-reform-packages/p4-passive-income-and-financial -taxes/.
7. Energy cost is higher in the Philippines than in Association of Southeast Asian Nations member countries that price energy at production cost, with no subsidies.
8. The pilot CRI will not engage private sector firms in strategic dialogue; rather, it will engage firms in the collection of information for the industry analysis.
9. The team will consider a one- to two-week online training to test the concepts being developed (the European Foundation for Cluster Excellence has done similar online training). This training will engage the Department of Trade and Industry and key stakeholders, while the team works to secure additional funding that could cover the other four to five weeks of training at a later stage.
10. Running the change management program through a public-private dialogue is a full-time job and will require hiring a consultancy to do the coaching and obtaining a strong

commitment from the Department of Trade and Industry. The process will take 8–12 months from the time the consulting firm is hired to completion.

REFERENCES

Acemoglu, Daron, and Paul Restrepo. 2019. "Automation and New Tasks: How Technology Displaces and Reinstates Labor." *Journal of Economic Perspectives* 33 (2): 3–30.

AVCJ. 2017. "Private Equity and Venture Capital Report: Southeast Asia." https://www.avcj.com/static/about-us.

Baller, Silja, Soumitra Dutta, and Bruno Lanvin. 2016. "The Global Information Technology Report 2016: Innovating in the Digital Economy." World Economic Forum, Geneva.

Bhalla, Vikram, Carl Harris, Dinesh Khanna, Xinyi Wu, and Alex Dolya. 2012. "Private Equity in Southeast Asia: Increasing Success, Rising Competition." Boston Consulting Group, Boston, MA. https://image-src.bcg.com/Images/BCG%20Private%20Equity%20in%20Southeast%20Asia%20Dec%202012_tscm108-101268.pdf.

Calì, Massimiliano, Martin Cicowiez, Aufa Doarest, Taufiq Hidayat, and Dhruv Sharma. 2020. "The Economic Impact of Investment Provisions: Evidence from Indonesia." World Bank, Washington, DC.

Gines, Ben Jr. 2021. "PNR Phase 1 on Track for Completion in 2022." *The Manila Times*, December 2, 2021. https://www.manilatimes.net/2021/12/02/news/regions/pnr-phase-1-on-track-for-2022-completion/1824370.

Government of the Philippines. 1936. "The Public Service Law, Commonwealth Act no. 146." Metro Manila.

Government of the Philippines. 1991. "An Act to Promote Foreign Investments, Prescribe the Procedures for Registering Enterprises Doing Business in the Philippines, and for Other Purposes, Republic Act no. 7042." Metro Manila.

Government of the Philippines. 2000. "An Act Liberalizing the Retail Trade Business, Repealing for the Purpose Republic Act no. 1180, as Amended, and for Other Purposes, Republic Act no. 8762." Metro Manila.

IMF (International Monetary Fund). 2020. "The Philippines: Financial Sector Assessment Program—Detailed Assessment of Observance—Basel Core Principles for Effective Banking Supervision." Country Report 2020/296, IMF, Washington, DC, November 2020. https://www.imf.org/en/Publications/CR/Issues/2020/11/10/Philippines-Financial-Sector-Assessment-Program-Detailed-Assessment-of-Observance-Basel-Core-49874.

Preqin. 2017. "Preqin Special Report: Asian Private Equity and Venture Capital." Preqin, London.

Tavares-Lehmann, Ana Teresa, Perinne Toledano, Lise Johnson, and Lisa Sachs, eds. 2016. *Rethinking Investment Incentives: Trends and Policy Options.* New York: Columbia University Press.

World Bank. 2020a. "Impacts of COVID-19 on Firms in the Philippines: Results from the Philippines COVID-19 Firm Survey Conducted in July 2020." World Bank, Washington, DC.

World Bank. 2020b. *World Development Report 2020: Trading for Development in the Age of Global Value Chains.* Washington, DC: World Bank.

www.ingramcontent.com/pod-product-compliance
Lightning Source LLC
Chambersburg PA
CBHW041448210326
41599CB00004B/182